D0331720

The Ultimate Audition Book
for Teens Volume XIII

111 One-Minute Monologues
-*Active Voices*-

THE ULTIMATE AUDITION BOOK FOR TEENS SERIES

The Ultimate Audition Book for Teens Volume 1: 111 One-Minute Monologues

The Ultimate Audition Book for Teens Volume 2: 111 One-Minute Monologues

The Ultimate Audition Book for Teens Volume 3: 111 One-Minute Monologues

The Ultimate Audition Book for Teens Volume 4: 111 One-Minute Monologues

The Ultimate Audition Book for Teens Volume 5: 111 Shakespeare Monologues

The Ultimate Audition Book for Teens Volume 6: 111 One-Minute Monologues for Teens by Teens

The Ultimate Audition Book for Teens Volume 7: 111 Monologues from Classical Theater, 2 Minutes and Under

The Ultimate Audition Book for Teens Volume 8: 111 Monologues from Classical Literature, 2 Minutes and Under

The Ultimate Audition Book for Teens Volume 9: 111 Monologues from Contemporary Literature, 2 Minutes and Under

The Ultimate Audition Book for Teens Volume 10: 111 One-Minute Monologues for Teens by Teens

The Ultimate Audition Book for Teens Volume 11: 111 One-Minute Monologues — Just Comedy!

The Ultimate Audition Book for Teens Volume 12: 111 One-Minute Monologues — Active Voices

THE ULTIMATE SCENE STUDY SERIES FOR TEENS

The Ultimate Scene Study Series for Teens Volume 1: 60 Shakespeare Scenes

The Ultimate Scene Study Series for Teens Volume 2: 60 Short Scenes by Debbie Lamedman

THE ULTIMATE MONOLOGUE SERIES FOR MIDDLE SCHOOL ACTORS

The Ultimate Monologue Book for Middle School Actors Volume 1: 111 One-Minute Monologues by Kristen Dabrowski

The Ultimate Monologue Book for Middle School Actors Volume 3: 111 One-Minute Monologues by L. E. McCullough

The Ultimate Monologue Book for Middle School Actors Volume 4: 111 One-Minute Monologues — The Rich, The Famous, The Historical by Kristen Dabrowski

To order call toll-free (888) 282-2881
for more information visit us online at www.smithandkraus.com

The Ultimate Audition Book for Teens VOLUME XIII

• • •

111 One-Minute Monologues
-*Active Voices*-

M. Ramirez

YOUNG ACTORS SERIES

A Smith and Kraus Book

ACKNOWLEDGMENTS

To drama teachers: Without them, where would all us dorks go? To Ana Mederos-Blanco, James Puig, Lizzy Silverio, and Minnie Perez. A very special thanks to Elsie Gattas, Lizzie Leeds, Manny Arca, Peanut, and Sarah Landman.

This book is dedicated to all my former students: Kateh, Alfie, Chenet, Ally, Kasbar, Multach, Noble, Berman, Gaby, Angeles, Gabriel, Siew, Sasso, Pedro, Cusco, and all the other punks I forgot. These monologues are your voices speaking, not mine. (Except for the really *good* voices, those are totally mine.)

Lastly, and most notably, perhaps, I'd like to thank Renata Russell. On more than one occasion this remarkable woman saved me from falling headfirst into a river of doubt. She taught me how to be a teacher, and more importantly, she taught me *why* to be a teacher.

I'm out.

—M

A Smith and Kraus Book
Published by Smith and Kraus, Inc.
177 Lyme Road, Hanover, NH 03755
www.smithandkraus.com

First Edition: January 2008
Manufactured in the United States of America
10 9 8 7 6 5 4 3 2 1

Cover and text design by
Julia Gignoux, Freedom Hill Design

ISBN 978-1-57525-581-1
Library of Congress Control Number: 2007942754

Introduction

So you're flipping through more than a hundred monologues, trying to find one before your brain explodes and it happens: for a second, you regret taking Drama in the first place. Yes, your friends who took Band have it so much easier. They get sheet music, they perform it, and they're done — but not you. No, you wanted to act, and what's worse: your teacher slammed you with a "Monologue" assignment for class.

But don't stress yourself too much. Turns out, Drama was a fine choice, and monologue performance isn't this long-lost crazy art form you can't do yourself.

You watch people do it all the time: David Letterman, that whiny kid in Science class, your Uncle Steve. Think of monologues as nothing more than stories. You've told stories, right? I mean, you don't give them titles, but you could, if you really had to: "The Thing That Happened at School Today," "The Day The Weird Guy at the Mall Talked to Marty." Any time you've ever told someone a really great story, any time you've stated your case, any time you've ever begged and pleaded for your parents to buy you something, for your teacher to change your grade, for the guy at the theater to let you sneak into a Rated-R movie, you've performed a monologue.

OK? So, moral of the story: You can do this.

More importantly: I think this book can help. (That was my pep talk.)

Casting directors' number-one complaint is that young actors don't choose age-appropriate material. I know what

Contents

you're thinking: "But I can play ANY age." Know what that response is? Cute. (Sorry, but it's true. Who would you rather have telling you the flat-out truth? Me, a random guy who wrote a book? Or a judge/teacher/casting director person: People who get PAID to judge you. Me. Right. Exactly.)

Think about it: These casting directors have to sit through tons of auditions where sixteen, thirteen-year-old young men and women are trying to play men and women in their thirties. Deep down inside, no matter how good these actors are, they can't escape that one fact: They're teenagers. And even if they DO play a wonderful thirty-year-old, the first thing on the casting director's mind is "But can this kid play a teenager."

There's no need to squeeze yourself into an adult character's shoes. You're a teenager. Why should you have to subject yourself to "playing" an adult?

Play a teenager.

The monologues in this book are specifically for actors thirteen to nineteen. Some of them are for young men, some are for young women, and some are for both. These are pieces that judges, teachers, and casting directors have never seen before. These monologues are active. They pop like nobody's business. They can be fun when they need to be fun. They can be poignant when they need to be poignant. These are stories only teens could tell, stories that'll make your ability really shine through.

These are the monologues you've been looking for.

There's obviously more to monologue picking than THIS IS THE BOOK, but the key — the only real piece of advice I can give you — is to not get overwhelmed. Pick the monologue that you can relate to. Pick the one that makes you laugh.

Pick the one that makes you cry. Pick the one you see yourself in.

Then, do your best to infuse it with life. Make your monologue ACTIVE. It's OK to sweat or to scream. Not every monologue calls for it, but what I mean is, try your best to stuff your monologues with energy, with motivation, with reality, and with ACTION.

Ask yourself some questions about your monologue and character: Who are you? Who are you talking to? Where are you? Is it raining outside? What do you want? What are you willing to do to get it? What are you NOT willing to do? What did your character have for breakfast? What does your character dream about?

Ask yourself other questions. Ask yourself better questions, and please, just make them yours.

Oh, and one last thing.

The stage directions, the stuff in parentheses, those are there to help you. Hopefully, they do, but I tried to not give you TOO much. There's some discovery you have to do on your own. This isn't paint-by-numbers acting.

You'll be fine.

You look like a smart actor.

At least, holding this book, you totally do.

— M. Ramirez

female · comedic

PAIGE WENT TO THE MALL

*Paige talks to Derek, her older brother's best friend.
She holds a plastic bag from a toy store. She's frus-
trated, and she very much wants Derek to know why.*

A *hundred* people, Derek! You said it would be no big deal
and you said I could just "walk-on-in-and-walk-on-out" but
I show up twenty minutes *early* and there are A HUNDRED
PEOPLE in line in front of me . . . You know what a HUN-
DRED people looks like? And they all want the same thing,
they all showed up, EVEN EARLIER THAN I DID, for the
release of some stupid toy, some stupid thing called the,
the— *(She reads the name from a crumpled piece of paper.)*
"the DELUXE GUNDO WING RESPONSE ANIME
ACTION FIGURE"
     (She drops the piece of paper.)
     And OF COURSE my brother wants one because he
COULDN'T WANT something REAL or something regular
like a T-shirt or concert tickets or *Back to the Future* on
DVD or anything, NO,
     Because *my* older brother is TWENTY-SIX and his
excuse for being
     UNENDINGLY SUPER WEIRD is
     (In the brother's voice.) "Paige . . . I collect toys."
     You should have told me, Derek.
     You should have warned me about those people.
     Those nerds. Those . . . toy people.
     They were in costumes, Derek.
     Grown people, in, costumes. At the mall. The last time I
was in costume at the mall it was Halloween and I was SIX
and yes I know that wasn't that long ago but I'm old enough
to know NORMAL from WEIRD, and those people, were
not normal.
     Yes I got one. No thanks to you and no thanks to the

three-hundred-pound woman in front of me in line who bought SIXTEEN.
And you know what it looks like?
A Barbie doll.
With an Anime face and a big bazooka ray-gun thing but still,
A Barbie doll, Derek.
Next year, my brother gets a gift certificate to Bed Bath & Beyond.
I hope he likes towels.

THE REGULAR-TYPE OPERATION

A young teenage girl describes a top-secret operation gone wrong, when she's serious, she's VERY serious, when she's smitten, she's VERY smitten.

It was a regular-type operation. Simple. Nothing special. Nothing out of the ordinary. The others had all their equipment ready and we had each made the necessary arrangements. We were ready. No . . . We were MORE than ready. We were PREPARED.

Bunny had called me and I phoned RedEagle and we were all waiting at our respective "rendezvous" points. "Rendezvous"? That's French . . . for "the place we were supposed to be meeting."

I like the French.

Our watches had all been synchronized. We were poised and ready for attack. And that's when it happened. That's when I saw him.

His name, I later found out, was Eric . . . IS . . . Eric. Such a silly name. Such a silly, silly, name. "Eric." So "blah," so "who cares," so . . . so "Little Mermaid."

But I don't think there is a name . . . that could properly describe "Eric" . . . That face. That nose. Those eyes . . .

I didn't know who he was, then I realized, our enemy had once mentioned an older brother. A detail that had completely slipped my mind. Sydney the Evil one HAD an older brother. Much older. Mature. Like sixteen. And not just any older brother.

Eric. A GOD among older brothers.

I couldn't go through with it. How do you egg the house of a person THAT handsome? How do you actually muster up the courage to approach Eric's front door and say "Hey, most handsome person that has like EVER existed, I'd like to throw a chicken fetus at your welcome mat."

The answer is easy. You don't.

ACTING CLASS

Angelique just got out of what she considers to be the worst acting class, ever.

I took an acting class and the teacher was this weird creepy guy who was going bald and who wore tight pants and didn't pronounce my name right ONCE.

ANGELIQUE. My name is ANGEL-EEK. Not "Angelica," not "Angie" . . . Angelique. It's French for "Like an Angel" or "Born from Angels" or "Touched by an Angel" . . . something. I dunno. It doesn't matter. He didn't get it right once.

He made us do all these weird creepy breathing exercises and all I could think of the whole time is MY MOTHER IS NOT PAYING FOR YOU TO TEACH ME HOW TO BREATHE, WEIRD CREEPY BALD GUY WITH TIGHT PANTS . . . MY MOTHER IS PAYING YOU TO TEACH ME TO ACT.

'Cause that's what I'm good at. Acting. Like I'm really good at swimming and I paint too and my sister and I made State Jazz Ensemble but what I'm REALLY good at? Is acting.

"Breathe in" . . . "Hold" . . . "Breathe out" . . . "Feel your inner animal reaching through" . . .

Inner animal? Are you kidding?

I Google-d the guy when I got home, whatever, I know it's weird, but I had to. I HAD to know what this guy's done that makes him so special.

Know what this guy's done, this guy who's supposedly gonna teach me how to act?

Three episodes of *Ghost Hunter Deluxe* and a deodorant commercial.

DEODORANT? Is this a joke? What's this guy gonna teach me to do? NOT SWEAT?!

JESSE EXPLAINS HOT GUYS

Jesse vents about hot guys and how horrible they are for a girl's self-esteem. Maybe she's venting to a friend who was just dumped. Or maybe Jesse was just dumped. Either way . . . here she goes.

'Cause he's hot, and that's just what hot guys do. They DON'T. CARE.

They walk around like they own the world and, well, let's be honest, they totally do, and they pick up and drop off girls like Blockbuster video games, only they don't pay late fees, they keep 'em around as long as they want, and when they're done, they just drop by the overnight box and slip 'em back in. Just like that. Like whenever they feel like it.

They're not real people. They're like cyborgs, but not really, 'cause cyborgs aren't really pretty. They're like androids. Is there a difference? Scratch that.

Whatever.

I'm dating ugly guys from now on. Fine. Not ugly guys, let's not go crazy, but not hot guys, that's for sure. No more nines, and definitely no more tens.

From now on, I date real people.

From now on, I date the guys that aren't on any teams, that aren't incredibly loaded, that aren't worried about who the next girl is that ends up in the drop box.

From now on, I date sevens, sixes, maybe even a five if he can play guitar.

THE DOLL MONOLOGUE

A doll complains about being abused by her owner.

Look at her. Look at her combing her hair. The cheat. The two-timing witch.

One minute, "OOH you're so beautiful" the next minute POOF. BOOM. You're gone. Back in the bin with all the other old toys, with the old crayons. With the cracked colored pencils and leftover LEGOS.

I hate December. That's when the newbies come in. That's when the new-and-improved versions come in, shiny plastic packaging and shiny plastic skin. Look at me. I look horrendous. It's 'cause of the sun exposure. Jenny left me in the SANDBOX last Sunday.

Can you believe that?

THE SANDBOX. I had to fight off two salamanders at the same time, while trying to find some kind of shade so my face and hair wouldn't fade, but look at me.

LOOK AT ME.

How am I gonna compete with those? With THAT? Have you seen her heels? They're gorgeous. Look what I'm wearing. Sooo last year. And ever since Jenny's friend Sarah decided on giving me a little haircut, well, let's just say I'm not the happiest camper.

I tried, I tried REALLY hard to warn her, SARAH I'M A DOLL THIS HAIR WON'T GROW BACK but do they listen? Do they ever listen?

Sometimes I feel like I'm not even here. Like they can't even hear me.

I thought I'd get lucky. I thought maybe they'd leave me in the box and I'd get to sleep it out for ten or twenty years and they'd sell me as a collector's item on eBay one day.

No such luck. Not for me.

Oh geesh, I hate December.

FLOWER GIRL (ZILLA)

The Flower Girl holds a bouquet and looks really stressed out.

No, Dena. I can't go get you an aspirin. And you know why? 'Cause Mary Ann and Joe are depending on me, 'cause their future kids are depending on me, the caterers and the priest and this whole wedding is depending on me.

'Cause I'm the Flower Girl.

I personally think I'm a little too old to be the Flower Girl but Mom says I'm also a little too young to be one of the bridesmaids, though Mary Ann IS my sister, and you've known her, oh, I dunno, EIGHT MONTHS.

But I'm fine with it. 'Cause Grandma and Uncle Clark explained something very important to me: at this wedding? There are four bridesmaids. And at this wedding, and at EVERY wedding, how many Flower Girls are there . . . ?

I KNOW THERE'S ONE THAT'S A RHETORICAL QUESTION (THOUGH YOU MIGHT NOT EVEN KNOW WHAT THAT MEANS 'CAUSE THOUGH I'M ONLY THIRTEEN I'M IN ADVANCED ENGLISH AND MAYBE SMARTER THAN YOU AND YOU WORK AT THE MALL).

Four bridesmaids. Four groomsmen. Five guys in the band playing the reception. Fifteen waiters. Eighty-three people in attendance at the wedding.

But you listen to me. There's only one . . . ONE . . . Flower Girl.

So you? "Dena"? "New friend"? "Mall girl"? "Brides-maid"?

You go get your own aspirin.

SOME HOBBY

*A girl tries to convince her mom to let her learn
another hobby.*

Mom, this isn't like the summer I wanted to take gymnastics.
Trust me, and this isn't like the time I thought maybe it'd be
cool to try singing lessons.

This is different.

This won't be just another thing and this won't be some
phase or some hobby I just do for like a week then give up,
and yes, I know I said that about the other things too, but
trust me, I mean it this time: I've never meant it more.

I've never meant *anything* more.

This isn't just a hobby we're talking about.

This is basket weaving.

And I might be good, I might totally suck, I might not be
able to weave to save my life, but that doesn't matter, Mom.
Sometimes the weave-y strand things get all tangled and
you're like AGGHH! I hate this but then you figure it out
and it all comes together and it all makes sense, not just the
basket, but your life. Our lives. The world. Everything.

I need you to understand that. This isn't about awards or
medals or telling Aunt Macy about how great I am when she
goes off on one of her things about Jenny . . .

This isn't for anyone else. This is for me. It feels right:
basket weaving.

The course isn't even that expensive. I've got like fourteen bucks saved up from babysitting. And I know it's not
that much, but it's something, it's something I can put
toward the one thing, that feels, right, that feels, like my calling.

This is different. I can do this.

(A beat.)

And the teacher's so hot.

WDXK

A young woman with her own pirate radio station
broadcasts revenge from her mother's basement.

Hello listeners, ladies, gentlemen, and most importantly, those under seventeen. You're listening to Katie, broadcasting live, L-I-V-E, from the basement of her mother's town house. You're tuned into W-D-X-K- Where the K stands for Katie, and Katie? Katie stands, for *you* . . .

In today's news, Mary Wilner lost her cat. She reported it to local authorities, but would like any help she can get from all you out there. Her cat, "Dolly," was black and tan, had beautiful green eyes, liked punk rock music, and is allergic to vanilla. Let's hope she's not allergic to car bumpers too, huh Mary? Kidding, I'm kidding, I really hope Dolly is fine. Though, well, I'm a dog person, myself. I mean, if I was driving and I had a choice, if there was a cute cocker spaniel on one side of the road, and, well, Dolly was staring up at me with her big green cat eyes, well, let's just say, "HELLO DOLLY," know what I'm sayin'?

In other news, Jaime Calahan's T-ball team beat Harry Wright's, and Harry's sister, Tiffany Wright, tenth-grade, has gained like thirty-three pounds in two months. All in her bra. No wonder the supermarket's runnin' out of tissues . . . huh Tiffany? Huh? I'm kidding, folks. Totally kidding. And so was Tiffany Wright when she said "I know you really like Brad, Katie, and I would never do anything to steal him from you" . . .

But that's enough of my petty nonsense, right? You want music, right listeners? Music music music. And so, let's keep it rolling, on WDXK, I'd like to dedicate this one to, oh, well, I dunno, Tiffany Wright.

Here's local band The Dirty Metal Spikes with their underground hit, "I Hate You So Much if a Car Landed on You I Totally Wouldn't Care" . . .

Don't change that dial.

CANDLES

A teenage girl thought the boy she liked would be into her, especially if she did all the specific romantic things.

I lit candles, Jenny, yes, I lit candles, just like you told me. But nothing.

He came over, he plopped his gear down, I made SURE he knew my parents weren't home, I made SURE he knew I was interested and we weren't going to get interrupted by my mom or my brother or my dog or anything — Yes, I locked Rusty in the garage. He loves the garage, it's like a second home to him, he just, he sniffs my dad's tools, he likes to get up and fall asleep leaning on Mom's old Bowflex machine — WHY ARE WE TALKING ABOUT MY DOG!

You told me if I thought he maybe liked me what I had to do was give him an opportunity to show it. And I did. I wore my hot jeans and everything — the ones with the thing on the side, yeah those — and NOTHING.

He was so cute on the car ride home, and so sweet, and so funny, he did his impersonation of Mr. Corradino, the math teacher with the tight shirts? And he didn't notice that I tuned the radio to "94.3 Smooth Hits You Love To Love," and it was all just wonderful.

And we walk inside, and we talked, and lit candles and I poured us some Diet Sprite, and, well . . . he . . . He played my brother's old Super Nintendo. The whole time. "I haven't seen one of these in years."

And I had to smile.

And I watched the wax drip. And then I just blew out the candles like it was a birthday party and the only one who showed up was me.

THIN MINTS

A teenage girl has come to sell Girl Scout cookies.
She hates it. She's way too tall for the outfit. Play it
monotone, sarcastic, TIRED, and annoyed.

Hello and good afternoon how are you fine thank you would
you like to purchase some Girl Scout cookies? We have new
low-carb options and this year, all our coconut cookies are
made from real organic coconuts from real organic coconut
farms like in Africa.
[The person asks a question.]
Sixteen. Why.
[The person asks another question.]
'Cause my mom says it's gonna look good on my college
applications 'cause all I got as far as extracurriculars go is
Drama and my Uncle Brad says only drug addicts and
democrats do "Drama." Do you want cookies or what?
[The person asks another question.]
No, I'm all out of "Thin Mints."
[The person asks a question.]
'Cause EVERYONE wants Thin Mints, what, you think
you're original? You don't look very original.
[The person asks a question.]
'Cause you drive a Toyota Camry and you look boring
now do you want cookies or what lady, 'cause I GOTTA
SELL COOKIES 'CAUSE I GOTTA GO TO COLLEGE
AND MY MOM SAYS IF I DON'T GO TO COLLEGE I'M
GONNA END UP ON THE STREET LIKE THAT GUY
WHO SELLS GIANT BALLOONS AND LIVES UNDER
THE FREEWAY, AND I DON'T WANNA SELL BAL-
LOONS AND LIVE UNDER THE FREEWAY —
[The person asks a question.]
— NO I DON'T HAVE THIN MINTS!

GORDON'S COMICS

A girl enters her older brother's room, terrified, to make this confession.

Gordon? . . . 'Member when you told me to that while you were gone you didn't want me in your room?
Well I'm sorry, but I came in.
Fine, yea, I know, I won't do it again.
No, that's not it.
'Member . . . when you told me that of all the places in your room, the most sacred was your collection of Green Lantern comics? The ones you keep in that big Tupperware container under your bed?
Well, I . . . I'm sorry, but I opened it.
I had to, I accidentally tripped on it. It was . . . totally an accident.
I know, just don't freak out, OK? Don't freak out . . . at least . . . not yet.
'Member? . . . 'Member when you told me that of all your Green Lantern comics, the one that really mattered, the one you'd burn yourself alive if you ever lost, the one that you sometimes liked more than your girlfriends, was that really old one, number six? . . .
Well . . . don't freak out . . . but what would you say if I told you that, completely by accident, it ended up at Janine's house . . . In the backyard . . . In her dog's mouth . . .
(She's nervous, but her brother starts laughing, it MUST be a joke.)
Hahhahaha . . . hahahaha . . . HAHAHAHA . . . oh geesh, yeah. . . wow . . . funny right? Haha . . . Gordon? . . . Why are we laughing?
[He answers, she must be kidding, right?]
I'm . . . Of course I'm kidding . . . It was Harriet's house . . . Janine doesn't have a dog she has cats and cats don't eat comics.

LIL' RED

Lil' Red is a ten-year-old rap star. Enough said.

It's hard, you know? It's hard out here, the rap industry, the rap industry don't even know! They don't even know! You think it's hard being a gangster? You think it's hard being a criminal out on the streets, in the rap game?

Imagine me! Imagine me man?! Imagine "Lil' Red" . . . ?

It ain't easy bein' a ten-year-old rap star, 'specially when you're a little cream-faced girl with blue eyes, man!

My first album sold twenty thousand copies in the first week. Da First Week! . . . Mostly 'cause of my hit single, "Little Red Riding in Da Hood." That jam was BUMPIN'.

But I rap about the life, you know? I rap about the struggle! I keeps it real! I rap about my problems, you know? Math homework, stale cafeteria food, gettin' detention, parties at Dandy Bear, it's REAL LIFE.

And that's what I'm about, I'm about "Real Life." That's the name of my second album. "I'm About Real Lyfe." Lyfe spelled with a Y . . . Why? . . . 'Cause I'm like that.

'Cause you meet a lotta rappers who fakin'. They STRAIGHT-UP-FAKIN, you know what I'm sayin? Talkin' bout "oh, it's hard out here on the street, the cops is so mean" . . .

COPS?!! COPS?!!!

BOY!!!

Go to Catholic school! Those nuns will teach you some excessive force! Those nuns will USE the rulers on you, man . . .

I gotta go but buy my third album . . . "Lil' Red: Return of the Red-eye" . . . see that's a Star Wars joke . . . man . . . I'm out.

BABYSITTING

An older sister has been left to babysit her younger siblings for the first time. The second mom and dad leave, she basically becomes a drill instructor.

SHUT UPPPPPPPPP! . . . Now listen and listen good, runts, 'cause I'm only saying this ONCE and if I have to say this TWICE I'll be using a lot of curse words and I don't WANNA use a lot of curse words 'cause Mom decided it'd be cute to do like on 7th *Heaven* and put that jar in the kitchen where we have to put a nickel in for every time we say "darn it" and a quarter in for every time we say something worse.
[One of the kids tells her she now owes a nickel.]
NO I DON'T HAVE TO PUT A NICKEL IN TIMOTHY I WAS JUST MAKING A POINT!!!! *(She controls herself.)*
Mom and Dad left me in charge, and this is a big deal, 'cause although you runts might not realize it, this is a big step for me. This is a step into adulthood, into womanhood, into real-person hood. This means they trust me. And I know only yesterday I was your sister and we were playing and watching *Little Mermaid* and having a jolly-old-time and coloring the walls with Crayola but TRUST ME! THAT TIME IS OVER.
FUN TIME . . . IS OVER.
While Mom and Dad are gone there will be no coloring, there will be no eating, there will be no leaving those chairs I've duct taped you to.
NO, this isn't a joke . . . No, this isn't a game. This is real life, children, and I intend to start being a real person, RIGHT NOW.
If you need me, I'll be upstairs, watching the restricted channels on Cable TV and jumping on the bed.
[Someone asks a question.]
'Cause I FEEL LIKE IT, DARN IT!
(A beat.)
I'll put a nickel in, later.

MY NEW HAIRCUT

A girl rushes onstage, her hair up in a bun, the bun covered with a big hat of some type.

You have to promise not to laugh, you have to promise me, you have to swear on your life that you're not gonna laugh . . . Is that a promise? OK . . .
(She takes the hat off, revealing a pretty nasty haircut, buns and ponytails all in odd places, making her look like a human Chia Pet.)
What? . . . what did you just say? . . . are you kidding? Is that a joke?
WHAT DO I *THINK* OF IT? . . . I THINK I LOOK LIKE A DISNEYLAND FIREWORKS DISPLAY, THAT'S WHAT I THINK.
I think if MURDER wasn't ILLEGAL, and explicitly forbidden in the Old Testament, I think I would've grabbed that hairdresser lady by the EARS and thrown her off a bridge! . . . A TALL ONE! . . .
Look at these ends! SPLIT?! SPLIT?!! LOOK AT MY BANGS!!! I look like a Yorkshire terrier who got run over by a lawn mower . . . THAT'S NOT FUNNY!
NONE OF THIS IS FUNNY! . . .
(She puts the hat back on.)
Maybe no one'll notice . . .
(She adjusts the hat.)
Maybe . . .
(It doesn't work.)
AGHGHGHGHG!!!

THE ONE ABOUT
THE WATER HEATER

A girl comes up to the bathroom door and knocks on it, holding a towel. Her brother's inside taking a WAY long shower.

Hey Jeremy how much longer you gonna be? . . .
[He answers, "Not much."]
Mom says you have to get out. She says you've been in there too long and you're gonna waste all the hot water and as it is the water heater's been acting up so yeah.
["What did she say?"]
THE WATER! She says you're gonna WASTE all the HOT WATER AND THE WATER HEATER'S BEEN ACTING UP SO YEAH!
(She walks over to the water heater.)
Is this thing old for a water heater? I don't know what new ones look like.

She says if you accidentally bump it, it turns off all of a sudden and the pipes come loose and you get nothing but freezing cold water from outside . . . and it's January . . . so . . . yeah.
["What?"]
I SAID IT'S JANUARY and anyways I need to take a shower too and do my eyebrows and my hair and exfoliate and a lotta stuff so get out . . .
[What?] I SAID I GOTTA EXFOLIATE SO GET OUT!!
[Why is she screaming?]
I'M NOT SCREAMING IT'S JUST . . . it's just you can't hear me 'cause you're spending too much time conditioning your stupid hair and the water heater isn't working too well.
[What?]
I SAID I'M NOT SCREAMING IT'S JUST YOU CAN'T HEAR ME 'CAUSE . . . I'M— UGH!— JUST GET OUT

AND STOP CONDITIONING YOUR STUPID HAIR
'CAUSE THE . . . cause the . . .
   (To herself.) If you accidentally bump it . . .
   *(She thinks about it, steps back, then kicks the water
heater once, really good. A guy's SCREAM from offstage.)*
Thank you.

THIS IS NOT A PARTY

Christina's parents have just come home a day early from vacation. They have rudely interrupted a party she was in the middle of throwing. She's nervous, making up every word.

I know what you're about to say, but don't worry about it, because I've got it covered. Completely. One hundred percent.

This, is NOT a party. I can give you a perfectly valid, academic reason why each of the thirty people that are here, are here. Every single one.

Yes. Even the kid dancing on the kitchen counter, with Ginger. Ginger! Get down from there! Come here, baby. What did that mean kid do to you, hm, baby? This is not what it looks like. Like, not one bit. This is actually a study session.

A loud one, but a study session. Math — History! History . . . Fine, you know what? This is community service. I know, it seems weird, but it's true. This is, you see, those kids in the pool? Thos're . . . They're poor kids. Kids, without pools. From poor countries. Really poor countries where people can't afford chlorine, so, the pools, they're . . . It's so sad, Mom. It makes me appreciate so much —

— And those kids, the ones in the living room, they're, they're, you have no idea, those kids, they're . . . deaf, YES! DEAF! That's why the music's so loud! AWESOME! They asked me to turn it up and I said, I mean, what do you say to a kid who — It's not their fault, you know? It's the same with the poor pool kids and the, the kids kissing on the couch, those kids are . . .

They're actually . . . they were born . . . joined at the lips? They're, actually . . . that's how they say hello where they're from . . . they're . . .

You know what? I should go to my room.

No, no, you know what? I'll get everyone out. Then, then I'll pick everything up.

Then — I'll go to my room.

Don't even worry about saying it.

. . . I . . . I have SOOO learned my lesson.

space bar. And a B+ in this class, to me, to my overbearing mother, a B+ in this class screams of one thing: Neanderthal. And I am *not* a Neanderthal. I am not *satisfactory*. I am, I have always been, more than that, better than that, above average and —

[The teacher snatches the test and changes the grade.]

Thank you, Mrs. Sherman. I told you I was a good judge of character, and you, YOU, are . . . Yes . . . I'll leave now.

I'M IN LOVE WITH
THE VIDEO-STORE GUY

A young lady tells us the story of the cute, nerd video store guy she's fallen for.

He's cute. But like nerdy-cute. But like not super-ew-gross-Internet-video-gamer-nerdy-cute. Just "nerdy-cute."
And he's got a job!! But not like a weird creepy job. Not like a butcher or a twenty-four-hour-convenience-store-clerk guy either. Just like a job. A cute job.
He works . . . at a video store.
I was returning one of those Olsen Twin movies which was totally embarrassing but it was my little cousin's 'cause she was staying over for the weekend 'cause her parents are getting divorced? I was returning one of those and I decided, on a whim, just, just because, that I wanted to go in and look around at the New Releases.
Fine. Fine you caught me. No whim. No "on a whim." I saw him checking me out through the window by the overnight movie drop-off box and I was like hello nerdy cute guy and so I walked in.
I walked every aisle. EVERY AISLE. Horror to comedy to action to sci fi to everything and he *wasn't budging!* I mean, he was looking at me. He was totally checking me out even more but he just, he wouldn't leave from behind the counter, but I stuck to my guns, 'cause my sister says never ever ever make the first move so there I was just hanging out in horror or sci fi or whatever it was just staring blankly forward and FINALLY!!!
"Hey, you need anything?"
Just like that. So cute. So adorable. So helpful. "You need anything?"

YES!! I'm thinking. YOU!!! IN MY ARMS!! AT THE
PROM!! AT MY WEDDING!!
But I play it cool I play it real cool and I was just like . . .
like . . . "Naw . . . "
(A beat. She smiles.)
He says I look like a young Audrey Hepburn. Do you
know who Audrey Hepburn is? . . . Me neither!

GOOD HUSTLE

*A soccer player explains to a new team member why
she hates the star defender, Katie Gibson. Everything
in CAPS is directed at the game.*

GOOD HUSTLE!! —
     — Yeah riiiight, that girl couldn't hustle her way out of
a paper bag —
     — GO TEAM —
     — God I hate Katie Gibson —
     — WOO! —
     — I just like can't stand her every time I see her on the
field I just want someone to kick her in the shins or just grab
her by her ponytail and —
     — WORK IT YEAH WORK IT HUSTLE! —
     — just ugh . . . She's the reason coach won't put me in,
we both play defender and he says we can't be on the same
field at the same time, he doesn't trust us —
     — WOO! —
     — And of course by "doesn't trust us" he means he
probably knows about my wanting to kick her in the shins or
grab her ponytail or whatever 'cause maybe I say that too
much but either way, he won't put us out there at the same
time —
     — STAY IN THE GAME BABY YEAH! —
     — And I know why that is, and it's real simple. Katie
Gibson's mom. Coach's got the hots for her. Ever since she
got that divorce, he's totally wanted her. You can tell in his
eyes. My mom says they were like high school sweethearts or
whatever but then she went away to college and he got stuck
here teaching Phys. Ed. And so he's wanted her like bad ever
since —
     — YOU CAN DO THIS YEAH GO TIGERS! —
     — So when he heard she got divorced, well, let's just say,

Katie Gibson didn't even really try out for the team. She just showed up one day in uniform like "Hey guys!" with that perky annoying voice thing she does just like "Hey guys!" and, well, the rest is history . . . Enter Katie Gibson. Exit me. Welcome to bench duty —
   — WOOOOOOO!!!
Please.
Please someone get her in the shins.

CAMP COUNSELOR

A bitter camp counselor screams at her "brats"
before putting them to bed.

Now listen up, brats.

This is a summer job, OK? Which implies it's temporary, OK? Which implies, my contract, or the duration of employment here, is, well, only a couple months long so, it's in no one's best interest to fire me.

Which means, basically: I'm completely in charge. Completely. And pesky phone calls to parents or petitions or letters to the owners of Camp Jimiwawa would only make things worse for you, trust me.

Now don't get stressed out. Camp Jimiwawa can still be VERY fun for you this year. Tons. However. I want no roughhousing, no name-calling, no staying up past bedtime, no loud music, no soft music, no reading of material inappropriate for those under eleven, no reading, no patty-cake, no hair braiding, no bonfires, no swimming, no diving, and absolutely no singing, under any circumstances, of "Kumbaya."

Now. If anyone needs me, I'll be in the boy's bunker with Brad Finley, senior counselor and cutest guy ever . . . We're gonna be . . . um . . . discussing . . . tomorrow's . . . activities.

Lights out.

SMOOTHIE PLACE

A young woman who works at a Smoothie Store asks for a raise.

Mr. Reno? Mr . . . Sir? Look. I've been meaning to speak to you. Look, I really like this job. Really. I really like using the blenders, making smoothies, peeling bananas, refilling the apple juice, really, this job really rocks. My friend Janine has this lame-o job at this rock-climbing gym, totally lame, I know. She even tried to get me to go there but I told her, "No Janine," just like that I told her, "Smoothie Place needs me, Mr. Reno needs me, the people who need their smoothies need me" . . .

So, you understand my sense of duty, my sense of, I dunno, "pathos," really, we learned that word in English, I think that's what it means, either way . . . You understand my regard for the work we do here. "We don't just make smoothies. We make you smile." And I really believe that. I really believe when I'm making someone the Berry Blast or the Super Strawberry Hurricane, I really believe I'm making them smile. Not today, maybe. Not in the store, not necessarily, but maybe when they get in their cars, maybe when they finish their smoothies, or, even, maybe weeks later, when they sit at their desks at their jobs and think about how good that Vitamin Vanilla smoothie tasted like twelve days ago, maybe THEN, maybe THAT's where they smile.

But either way, Mr. Reno, the reason I bring this up, is, well, I was wondering if I could get a raise. I've been with the company, oh, I dunno, five months now, and minimum wage plus tips isn't stretching the way it used to. Inflation's a tricky little monster, isn't it . . . I dunno what that means, my grandfather says that.

Either way, I was wondering, Mr. Reno? Whaddayasay? . . .

OATMEAL ZIT-CREAM COMMERCIALS

A young woman vents to a friend about not getting parts in commercials she's auditioned for.

Just, anything, Tina. ANYTHING would be good at this point. I keep going on these castings, these, GODAWFUL commercials for oatmeal and zit cream and, it's just, I mean when you DON'T get one of those gigs, when you don't even get CALLED BACK, it's just like, "What, I'm not good enough for zit cream?"

Is that what they're saying? I'm not a good enough actress to say "Look how my face cleared up!" . . . I played Ophelia . . . I don't need some loser casting director telling me I can't sell zit cream. I CAN SELL IAMBIC PENTAME-TER! Do you think a casting director even knows what that means?!

What, I didn't SMILE wide enough when I put the oat-meal in my mouth at auditions? Is that it? You wanna know why? 'CAUSE THE OATMEAL STINKS . . . 'CAUSE I HAD TO SPOON THIS GARBAGE INTO MY MOUTH, THIS CHOLESTEROL-FREE MAPLE-SYRUP FLAVORED GARBAGE, AND IT WAS COLD, AND IT TASTED LIKE CARDBOARD, COLD CARDBOARD, AND I JUST — . . .

(She recovers.)

It's just frustrating, I guess, is all I'm saying. I eat oat-meal, Tina. Right? I do. And I use zit-cream. You've seen me. It's not like I don't enjoy these products . . . it just . . . it sucks to get told I'm not even good enough to PRETEND enjoying them.

(A beat.)

Just . . . anything.

PROM DRESS

A girl drags her loser brother out to get a prom dress.

Button it up . . . Then zip it up, whatever it is, do it.
There. How's that look. "Like a dress" isn't helpful,
Steven, how does it look?!
    You should've just stayed home. Dad would've let me
take the car, you didn't have to . . . Don't ACT like you had
anything else better to do 'cause when I found you, when I
brought you your keys and your wallet you were on the
hammock outside reading comics . . . "Graphic novels,"
whatever . . . you were reading picture-books on the hammock outside and not really doing anything exciting at all
on a Saturday, which, I guess, comes as no surprise 'cause
you're twenty-six years old and kind of a loser but whatever,
I needed a ride.
    This isn't just any dress, Steven. This is my prom dress.
You'd know how important that was to me if you would've
GONE to your prom . . . Oh shut it, "I didn't wanna go to
my prom" is something losers say, losers who couldn't find
dates.
    It just sucks that Tina and Jessie are both outta town and
I gotta come with YOU. How's it look. Be honest. "Uhmm"
is not a response, Steven.
    Is it cut too low? Does it make my hips look wider than
they already are? My butt? Does it look big? Good-big? Bad-
big? Bubbly? What?
    Basically, if you were George Levine would you think I
looked cute in this . . . George Levine the lacrosse player.
Yea, Jan Levine's little brother . . .
    "Nice" . . . I look "nice"? . . .
    (A beat, genuinely touched.)
    Really?

TRICK OR TREAT

Rebecca enters, maybe seventeen. She's in a Halloween costume that looks like it should be on a nine-year-old, maybe the hat is on only half on her head, maybe it's got a cape or something, over her T-shirt and jeans. She holds out a paper bag. A beat.

What . . .

(Another beat, with attitude.)

I'm not gonna say it just put candy in there and lemme get outta here . . .

(Another beat.)

Look lady I said I'm not gonna say it.

I'm seventeen. I'm too old for this junk but my neighbor, Mrs. Hollinger, her son got the flu or chicken pox or something and so he's sick and in bed but he was crying about not being able to get any candy so his mom called my mom, my mom put me on the phone, and, well, Mrs. Hollinger slipped me some a couple bucks and . . . And I'm here . . .

(Another beat, she holds the bag out again . . .)

Do it.

The only reason I'm wearing the costume is, it'd just be begging otherwise . . . at least, if I've got this stupid thing on it's more like Trick or Treating, though it's just oozing with lameness all over, I know . . .

No. That's a stupid question. No, I've never had chicken pox, why.

(Suddenly worried.)

Ohmygod.

(She tears the stupid cape and hat away, slamming them on the floor.)

OHMYGOD OHMYGOD OHMYGOD OHMY—

(She runs off.)

female · dramatic

WATER, NO ICE

A girl talks to her boyfriend, who has been scouted by a major university's athletic program. She knows he'll leave soon, and she is just realizing it.

You shoulda seen 'em, Walter. The scout. Stopwatch in one hand, notebook in another. Real fancy suit.

He talked to me at the lemonade stand. He asked me for water. No ice. Just like that. "Water, no ice."

I think he liked you. I really do. The way he was lookin' at the way you were movin' out there, he looked real happy. Real excited like. I saw him on the phone later. Didn't hear what he was sayin', but I saw him. He was smiling at least.

I think you got a real shot. I do. Everyone says it. You're gonna . . . you're gonna be real famous soon. A big deal, playin' pro. Signin' autographs, drivin' nice cars, datin' models who weigh like twelve pounds.

You will. No joke. You will.

You're . . . I know you're outta here, Walter. I know you . . . I know you could say one thing or another but I know come June or July when those offers start comin' in . . . I know thing's'll change.

You won't change. Not you. But things will. Just . . . things.

You got bigger stuff out there waiting for you. You got . . . you got a whole world ready to just take you in with open arms.

And that . . . that's what, compared to me? High school sweetheart? Prom date? A cute-enough girl with an average GPA and a soft spot for vanilla milkshakes? Cute-enough.

I think he liked you. I really do. He was smiling. And that means you're gone.

FISTS

A girl describes her father's habits, and her father's job.

We used to have this joke, running between Dad and me. About these fist things? Anytime he was hiding something, anytime he was lying or kidding or something, he couldn't help it, it was like a nervous thing, he'd make a fist. Left hand, right hand, it didn't matter.

My sixth-grade surprise party? I totally figured it out, cause of the fist thing. I knew we weren't going to the movies. I knew 'cause he acted like he forgot it was my birthday but, but he did the fist thing, so, it was cute, so I knew. I figured it out whether I wanted to or not.

(Her emotions change, almost an explosion.)

You know what it was like to sit in there? To stand and watch him? It was . . . it was unbearable, Denise. Just like totally unbearable. There he is, in his suit, looking just like he does when he leaves the house. Looking, normal, right? Except he's not normal. He's not my dad. He's like . . . this other guy . . . he's in, "other guy" mode. He's at work, right?

And he's walking back and forth and he's talking to those people, the jury, or whatever, and he's talking like details about the case he's working on, he keeps looking at the guy he's defending, this real creepy-looking guy who supposedly did all this awful stuff, my dad's there talking about it, about how this creepy-looking guy DIDN'T do any of this stuff, and at first I'm like totally interested 'cause my dad's like in action and nonstop talking and he's really good at it . . . but he's got his hands closed, like in a fist.

And I know what that means, because what that means is . . . Something horrible.

And that's what my dad does for a living . . . And I figured it out whether I wanted to or not.

THE QUAKE AND SOMETHING SOLID

A young teen describes her (or his) first earthquake.

At first, everything was still. Nothing moved. Not a sound. Maybe a siren in the distance, maybe a car horn or someone screaming down the side of their building 'cause someone forgot their keys. Sounds like that. But not real sounds. Just . . . the usual. It was late. It was late and everything seemed normal. And I stared up at those cheesy "star" lights my sister put on the ceiling of our room when we were like five.

And I wasn't really thinking about anything. I was just waiting for sleep to come.

And suddenly everything was shaking.

My bed. The closet. Stuff on my desk, the floor, everything. Just . . . everything that isn't supposed to move, was moving. There wasn't anything solid anymore. It was like the whole world turned to liquid, there was nothing really you could count on. I mean, they say stand in doorways, but still, the shock . . . this was my first one . . . It was liquid.

It took me hours to recover. I felt dizzy. Not 'cause of the shaking, just . . . just everything felt unsafe. Everything felt . . . alive in ways I had never thought of before.

I started thinking about the world, not like a place where we live, but like, like another one of us, like it was shivering, like it was scared, like even IT didn't want to shake.

Like even IT wanted something solid.

RUSTED WHEEL

A have-not teen describes her mother's sad philosophy.

He says he's bound to win but Ma says he ain't goin' anywhere. Sometimes I think it's true and Ma's right. He just
ain't.

There are two kindsa people in this world, man. There's
people who do stuff, make decisions, get jobs, go to college,
eat expensive dinners, have coffee in little café's with their
pretty friends and nice expensive sweaters . . . And then
there's the rest of us.

The rest of us who eat microwave dinners and watch TV
and don't really do nothin' new or exciting or fresh, the rest
of us who don't never even leave where we came from not
'cause we don't want to, but just 'cause. 'Cause we never get
the chance. 'Cause we're just not the type of people who got
somewhere to go.

The way Ma says it, I think we're just that. The *rest*. The
people who don't really do nothing.

You think he's goin' anywhere? You can hope and pray
and dream all you want, but you think he's really gonna win
that stupid race and get some stupid prize money and get
outta here? You think that, you got another thing comin'.

You got disappointment comin', that's what.

He's a rusted wheel. And rusted wheels don't go no place.
Unless you push 'em hard enough.

(With hope in her voice.)

Unless . . . you really really push 'em.

ALMOST NO CARS

A girl who lives in the middle of nowhere, alone with her mother who runs a gas station, tells us the story of the last lady who came through. A somber, quiet, introspective monologue.

Almost no cars go passed here anymore. Used to. When there was that big steel mill thing up the road there. Where Dad used to work. But that place closed, they went away. And so did Dad. And no cars go passed here anymore. Just . . . Well hardly none.

A little while back a lady came through, said she was looking for her brother, showed me a picture, asked if I'd seen him. I hadn't. I said I was sorry, asked her if she needed gas. She didn't. She kept going. She looked like she hadn't slept in months. She smelled like vanilla and perfume.

Seems stupid, don't it? Real stupid. Mom owning a gas station that no one comes to? I mean, you figure *somebody's* gotta need gas. But they take alternate routes now, they got other places to be . . . Not here . . .

Except for that lady.

I think about her sometimes. I hope she found her brother. I think about whether or not she'll find him, about whether or not she'll hug him when she does, about what he looks like, probably much older than in the picture, about what she'll tell him. "I've been looking everywhere for you. I mean everywhere. Louisville. Reno. Everywhere. I even met this girl at this gas station."

I wonder if they'll sit down and have coffee, or wine, or whatever . . . I wonder if I'll be the first thing she tells him about.

JANITOR'S CLOSET

*A girl's friends have just jokingly stuck her in a jani-
tor's closet at school . . . And she has reason to freak
out. She pounds on the door, calling to her friends.*

OK come on . . . Hello? Anyone? Anybody? Hello? . . .
Shawn? Jason? This isn't funny. This isn't cool. I'm claus-
trophobic. Haha OK I get it very funny "let's shove her in a
janitor's closet" very funny very cute now open up.
    Come on . . . Open the door. Please? Come on I'm get-
ting really ticked off now. This place is creepy. This closet is
way creepy and you know why and I don't wanna be in here.
Please. Open the door. I'm afraid of tight spaces but I'm even
more afraid of the dark, and of ghosts. This isn't funny like
at all and I don't even know anybody who's gonna think this
is funny they're all just gonna think you're cruel and idiots
and Jason when everyone finds out what a cruel idiot you are
Regina Tyler'll never ever like you . . . Please open the door.
    (She gets increasingly freaked out.)
    OPEN THE DOOR NOW PLEASE OPEN THE DOOR
we've all heard the stories are you complete idiots?! Are you
insane? I know you heard the same stories I did about the
girl in the sixties or the seventies or whatever, my brother
told me and Jason I know Danielle must've told you something at some point so I KNOW you know . . . please please
please open that door.
    (She's almost hysterical now.)
    She died in here Shawn! Do you hear me?! SHE DIED IN
HERE! THIS ISN'T FUNNY. THIS IS TOTALLY CREEP-
ING ME OUT OPEN THE DOOR. PLEASE IT'S COLD IN
HERE AND I HEAR SOMETHING BEHIND ME PLEASE
THERE'S SOMETHING BEHIND ME PLEASE OPEN THE
DOOR LIKE RIGHT NOW PLEASE PLEASE THERE'S
SOMETHING IN HERE SHAWN!
    (She sits on the floor, in tears.)
    I know you heard the stories . . . I heard the stories . . .

NOT GOING BACK

A friend talks to another teen, one who gets picked on a lot at school.

Look, I know they're mean. I know they're stupid and they said stupid things. I know they hurt you and I know I can say "I know how it feels" but, let's be honest, I don't. I don't know half of what you've gone through and to say "I feel your pain" would be, well, just as insulting as the names they call you in there.

But I'll tell you what I know for sure. And what I know for sure is, ever since the first day you walked into that classroom, since the first time we all saw you, I didn't know you too well, I'm not even sure I liked you, but I respected you.

I respected you 'cause you ARE who you ARE and you're pretty proud of it. 'Cause it's been six months since the first day you walked into this school and you still haven't changed. Not one bit.

I respect you 'cause you're strong . . . strong in ways I only wish I could be . . .

And I understand if you don't wanna go back, if you don't ever want to walk into that room ever again, I'll go in there and get your stuff and bring it out to you . . . but I just want you to know . . . every day, watching you be as strong as you are . . . it makes me . . . it makes me proud . . . It makes me proud to be your friend . . . and it makes ME want to be stronger . . .

So no, I don't know how it feels to be you, you're right. I don't know what it's like to take all the trash they dish out, but I DO know how it feels to be me.

I DO know how it feels to watch them dish it, to watch you take it, to watch you throw it back in their faces.

I DO know how it feels to watch you walk in, every day, and beat them at their own stupid game.

And it feels wonderful.

ROOTLESS TREE

A girl tells us the story of a creepy tree in front of her house.

There was this tree when we moved in. This big, old, creaky thing. Huge. Dark. Like a tower with branches . . .
At night, the wind would howl and the leaves on it would make the most creepy sounds, like ghosts were whispering in through my room. Gives me goose bumps still.

At first I thought I could handle it, but I couldn't. I thought I was old enough and grown up enough, but I couldn't. There came a point when I couldn't sleep at all. It was just creaking, and creeping, and moaning, and whispering . . . the worst sounds . . . the most terrifying thing.

I remember the night I walked into my parents' room. It was maybe three in the morning. They were both asleep. I stood there, waiting, thinking maybe one of them would just wake up and I didn't actually have to go bother them. But they didn't. I stood there like forever and they didn't budge . . . so eventually . . . I had to say something.

I nudged my mom, or my dad, I'm not sure who, I don't remember, but I nudged one of them. They asked me what was wrong. "The tree outside." That's all I said, like that should explain everything. Of course, they had no idea what I was talking about.

"It's scaring me to death. And I wish it were gone."
(A beat.)
The next morning, my dad, my brother, and two of the neighbors got chain saws and axes and even a big jug of gasoline ready. They were gonna rip this thing to shreds, this . . . this monster. They were gonna tear out every root and burn the stump to make sure it never, ever grew back.

My brother cut through half of it, the thing collapsed,

and that was it. They looked at it like it was some kind of puzzle.

Turns out the thing had no roots. None at all. It just fell down. Like that. So easy.

As they chopped the thing down to nothing, as they made it nothing more than tree slices, really, I remember watching from my room, and I remember feeling sorry.

Feeling bad for it. This big old, creaky thing. Poor thing.

It was dying the whole time.

AUGUST, THE ONE WHO PAINTED

*August is a young woman with a gift for painting.
Gift is the wrong word — she's a genius. Her art
teacher at school has encouraged her tons, but
August wants to stop. She holds a handful of paintbrushes.*

I'm not . . . I don't want this. This . . . thing . . . I don't
want to be good at this.

I want to be regular, I don't want people to stare and
point and gawk and be like "oh look at that kid wow she's
so good" you know? Like "for a kid, wow, it's amazing, I
wonder where she gets it, I wonder where she gets that tal-
ent, maybe her mom, maybe her dad, I wonder who her dad
is, maybe he's some famous painter, yea, that's where she
probably gets it."

'Cause my dad isn't some famous painter. 'Cause my
mom's a waitress a diner that never closes and my dad's
trash . . . He's just . . . he walked out on us a long time
ago and he beat her and he gambles and he does . . .
things . . . that I don't wanna talk about because they're
disgusting and because he's my dad, which means — poten-
tially — I've got the potential inside me to, to be as disgusting as he is . . . at least . . . half of me . . . and even half of
me is bad enough . . .

I don't want people to stare at me, my paintings, anything, I don't want people to ask questions.

I don't wanna be some cute circus freak sideshow to anyone, or to anybody . . .

I'm just . . .

I don't wanna be the girl who made it out of "such a
tough life" cause . . . I mean . . . my mom doesn't need to be
reminded . . . she knows . . . she realizes every day that it's
tough . . . and she does her best and . . .

I don't want this . . .

(She holds out the paintbrushes, then places them on a table, takes a step back.)

I'm really . . . I'm sorry. But I'm never painting anything . . . ever again.

SILENT TREATMENT

A young woman (or man) has just pulled her (or his) first major betrayal, and she (or he) is now more sorry than she or he has ever been. A car ride home, Dad won't say a word.

Talk to me. Say something. Please? Don't give me that . . . don't give me some silent treatment thing . . . Just . . . just say something.
    (A beat. Waiting. Nothing.)
    This is worse than being grounded, would you just ground me? PLEASE! Come on . . . something? Say something?!!
    (A beat.)
    I'm sorry. Is that it? Is that what you wanna hear? I'm sorry, OK Dad? Now say something.
    (A beat.)
    What more do you want? What more do you want from me? I said I'm sorry and I meant it and I'm begging you to please just Dad just please . . .
    I didn't . . . I didn't think. OK? I wasn't thinking. I was stupid and it's totally TOTALLY my fault and it was, it was, well whatever it was just stupid. I was being . . . I was just stupid . . .
    Jerry said he wouldn't tell anybody and so did Sarah and it's not like I'm trying to push the blame anywhere it's just . . . the worst part of the whole thing is that . . . is that you asked me and you told me you wouldn't get mad and you told me just to be honest, just, just to be honest with you . . .
    . . . and I lied to you.
    And I'm . . . Sorry isn't even the word anymore, Dad . . . I'm . . . Please . . . please say something . . .

ONE TIME I HAD A WATCH

A kid talks about her (or his) mom's job, and the bus ride home.

My mom used to clean hotel rooms, like, like it was her job, she'd clean hotel rooms. Whenever there was a day off school or something I'd go in with her, 'cause she didn't want me alone at home 'cause she thought the kids in the neighborhood were "hoodlums" — which, which they were, but they were still my friends.

She had this routine. Knock, knock. "Housekeeping." Then she'd open the door, we'd go in there. First thing out was the towels, then the sheets. Then she'd wipe down tables, dust the TV, maybe vacuum. Put the cups and the ice bucket in the perfect position, fold the new towels, all that stuff. She was good. It was like a science. I was in her way, mostly. Then at the very end of it all she'd open the windows for a second, let the brightness and the air in, and she'd say "Nice, huh?" Every time. Every room. "Nice, huh?"

Sometimes the people'd leave tips. Sometimes not. It didn't bother her either way. She'd pick it up, three dollars, sometimes more, sometimes less, sometimes some change, she'd pick it up like it was trash, like old towels and leftover room-service pancakes.

The tips were OK, but every so often she'd find things. Sometimes she'd bring them home to me. Once she found some shoes. Another time a calculator. If no one would come back to claim it by the end of her shift, she'd take it home.

One time I found this watch. She let me put it in my pocket, but she told me, if someone came to claim it by four thirty, that was the end of her shift, if someone claimed it by then, I'd have to give it back.

I never had a watch before. I could tell time now. Four came. Four ten. Four twenty-five. Nobody came . . . Then this kid comes running down the hall. Maybe a year older than me, maybe younger, I dunno . . . I was close . . . My mom didn't say much. She finished her last room. She opened the windows. She came close to me, I could smell the soap and clean towels on her. She waved her hand like she was showing me the room, like it was the first time I'd ever seen bright sunlight creep in through blinds and hit a perfectly made bed.

"Nice, huh?" *(A beat.)*

At four thirty we took the bus home. At least I guess it was four thirty. I couldn't tell the time anymore. But that was OK . . . I liked it better that way.

I SAID I WAS SORRY

A young woman was approached by a homeless woman. She tells us the story.

Yesterday a woman came to me.

She looked real tired, worn out. Dry skin, cracked lips. She was wearing slippers over socks which is weird 'cause it was forty, maybe thirty degrees outside.

She didn't look at me in the eyes, she looked behind my shoulder first. Like maybe there was someone behind me, like she was hiding from someone or from everything.

At first I was afraid but there was something about her that made me think she was somehow more than just some crazy lady. Like the slippers over socks and the cracked skin and the cold eyes were a costume she was wearing, like if I could peel all those back there was a lady just like Mrs. Matheson my Science teacher, or Aunt Rose, or someone normal.

I was about to cross the street but she looked at me like she had something very important to say, like she was gonna tell me my future, like I couldn't go another second without hearing whatever it was she had to say. I reached in my pocket and felt two quarters there and told myself I'd hand them to her and keep walking soon as she asked me for money.

She came closer, stepped in a cold wet puddle, which must've felt horrible but you couldn't tell from the look on her face.

She asked me if I'd seen her son.

I said no. I looked around. I didn't see any son anywhere. But I realized she wasn't asking like a woman at the grocery store looks for her son. She wasn't asking like he was most likely in the next aisle picking up his favorite cereal.

She asked like she hadn't seen him in years.

I said no again. I said I was sorry.

And I was. I was so, so, sorry.

CLOUD STUFF

A short piece for a dreamer, someone who'd rather be somewhere else.

You ever see stuff in the clouds? Just . . . stuff? Faces? Boats? Little ducks with cheeseburgers in their mouths? Smiling? Like "Hey, I sure like cheeseburgers . . . quack" . . .
    You ever spend a whole afternoon, just lookin'?
    You ever see — You ever see a fluffy white whale like swallowing something kinda shaped like Mexico? A piece of corn on the cob floating on a sea of Tic-Tacs? Babies? Fat babies, wrestling one another, little tufts of white cotton smoke coming out of their ears, like they're really mad, or really hot, or really *something*?
    Whole afternoon, just lookin'?
    No homework. No brothers. No sisters. No mom no dad no grandma no TV no Coke machines no expensive jeans no car accidents no buses no text messages . . .
    Just . . . you . . . and . . . the stuff in the clouds . . .
    Whole afternoon . . . Makin' you wish you could keep lookin' way into the night, makin' you wish you could still see what shapes are passing over you at two, three in the morning, when you could REALLY look, when you could REALLY just spend hours looking and no one would see you and it'd just be you and this whole . . . this whole world.
    That's what it is up there. A whole world.
    A better one.
    The one I think we're supposed to be living in.

FIRST ROOMMATE

A seventeen-year old girl talks to her older brother,
who's about to go away to college.

Done packing? . . . Early flight, right? Cool . . . Have
a . . . have a good flight, OK?
(She goes to leave, stops herself, thinks, for a while,
comes back.)
Danny? . . . Can I . . . You're not busy right? I know,
just, gimme a, just . . .
(She clears her mind, starts again.)
I know you and I have our . . . "things." I know, we
don't always get along 100 percent, I know I've, been a pain
sometimes, and you know, you have too. I know we don't
get along as well as Kara and Stevie do, I know we don't talk
about important stuff, or even unimportant stuff. We just . . .
we don't.

I know basically, that if you and I weren't like brother
and sister, there's no way we'd ever really say two words to
each other. And I don't mean that in a bad way, it's just, it's
true, right? Right.

But tomorrow you're gonna get on that plane and you're
gonna be gone and you're gonna be enjoying like EVERY
SECOND out of this house and I'm gonna be SO JEALOUS,
and you're gonna be living your freshman year at college and
you're gonna be too cool to call and yeah, you'll come home
for Thanksgiving and summer, but . . . but starting tomorrow it won't be the same. And I'm not an idiot. And I get
that.

And I realize you and I aren't gonna bicker over the cap
on the toothpaste, and you and I aren't gonna randomly see
each other at parties once a month and be all like "agh, why
do we have friends in common," and I realize I'm not gonna
have to knock on the bathroom door at seven AM 'cause

you're taking too long shaving around your stupid goatee . . .
And all that stuff . . . sounds . . . wonderful.

But . . . I wanted to tell you. . . . . . . I'm gonna miss
you. A lot. Even though we have our "things" . . . even
though you've basically made my life hell, and I've done the
same, for as long as I remember . . . The fact that you leave
tomorrow is really not something I'm as excited about as I'd
thought I'd be. Just . . . just wanted to say that.

When you're meeting cool new people and cool new room-
mates don't take too long shaving your stupid goatee . . . OK?
And don't forget who your first roommate was.

I CAN DO THIS BY MYSELF

Worried, Veronica answers the door to her small apartment. It's the landlord, Mr. Livingston, he's asking for her mom.

No, she's — my mom's asleep. Why? What do you need? She's tired . . . I dunno when she's gonna wake up, she had to work a double shift at work again and, and, I'll tell her to call you in the morning —
[He insists.]
She's ASLEEP, I TOLD YOU . . . She might . . . she might . . . she might've come in through the back door, or the fire escape, she does that, you sure you didn't see her? Well. Anyways she doesn't like to be bothered. If it's about the rent, I'll have it, SHE . . . she'll have it to you by the first, I promise . . . No it's not, I put it in your box already, I put it in the . . . she, Mom sent me to put it in the slot thing so I do as she told me, I'm just a kid, you know . . .
[He asks how old she is.]
Thirteen. Fourteen next November . . . Why? . . .
[How old is your little brother?]
Richie's seven. My brother, he's seven. Why do you have so many questions, listen, I told you my mom's asleep, she doesn't like me talking to strangers and I know you're the landlord, you're not just a stranger . . .
[I know your mother's not home.]
And what do you mean by that? . . .
[I know your mother's in jail again.]
No she's not. My . . . who told you that. WHO TOLD YOU THAT?! Who LIED TO YOU 'CAUSE I'M GONNA FIND THEM WHO TOLD YOU THAT — Maria told you that didn't she? MY MOM'S NOT IN JAIL! SHE'S NOT! SHE'S NOWHERE! SHE'S NOWHERE BUT IN HER BED, RIGHT NOW, and I'm gonna make some macaroni and

cheese and Vienna sausages for dinner cause that's Richie's favorite and it only comes out to like a dollar ninety for the whole thing . . .

(Suddenly desperate.)

Do you know what they'll do to us . . . They'll separate us, Mr. Livingston, they'll split us up, and I don't want that. I can't have that. Richie, see, he's . . . he's not a hundred percent "there," you know? I mean he's smart at lots of stuff, you know, but not like the commonsense stuff, like tying his shoes, you know? He's seven but he can't tie them yet, most kids tie them by like four or five but, he's . . . he needs me to do stuff like that for him, and it's not too much, and I can handle it, and Mom'll be back soon, she promised, she calls on the phone and tells me to put all the whites in the wash together and I can handle it, Mr. Livingston, I can handle it just fine . . . Please . . . I can handle this . . . I'm . . .

(A beat, she takes a breath, now desperate.)

I'm doing just fine.

GHOST STORIES

Whoever tells this story should tell it intensely, remembering even the details that aren't in the monologue, whatever those are.

I used to live in this house on Ferry Hill, this big, overgrown place. The planks of wood would creak every chance they got, the doors would squeak no matter how much we oiled the hinges, no matter how often we tried, even after replacing the whole doors, they still squeaked, like that was what they were supposed to do.

I don't . . . I don't like talking about this very much. I . . . I don't like the way it makes me feel, like an aching weird pain in my stomach, and I'm . . . I guess I'm kinda afraid of how you're gonna look at me after I tell you this . . . But . . .

There was . . . this room. My mom used to talk about how she wanted to make it like a home office or a playroom or something for my sister, but she never did. We never got around to it, she said, but I knew why. I knew why she kept the key to that room hidden in her bedroom closet.

The first time I heard it I was like four years old. But as I got a little older, I realized something was very weird.

Other kids' houses didn't have one empty room in their houses that sounded like crying in the middle of the night. Other kids had monsters under the bed, in the closet, all that cute storybook stuff. No one I talked to had a room that the whole family was afraid to talk about.

We moved last summer. I decided . . . I decided I had to know. I had to try. The boxes were all packed, all our stuff was on its way out, each room had just like a bed and a lamp in it, the movers were gonna take that the next day. It was a gamble but — sure enough — there it was, in my mom's bedroom closet. The key to the room I had been prepping myself, psyching myself out to go into for years. I don't wanna tell you what I saw when I walked in. I don't wanna tell you what it looked like, or what it sounded like up close, or what it said to me. You probably wouldn't believe me even if I told you. I don't . . . I don't like talking about this very much. People look at you differently when you tell them ghost stories. Especially true ones.

MUD

The young woman is helplessly in love. The world she lives in, however, doesn't allow for luxuries like that.

Sometimes I'd think about different ways to talk to him. To communicate, you know? They kept him locked up pretty tight, "they," the people in charge, but there had to be a way. There's always a way, there's always, something. Something they hadn't thought of. At least not yet. So I went by. I had to. I snuck out one night, just, got up and I went by, wondering, wanting, no, NEEDING, to see him. I avoided the front door 'cause that's where the guards were and I went around the back in an alley, near the west side of the building. I waited. I sat in the mud. I've always been patient. Very patient. At least, when I know something's for sure. An hour passed. I stayed there, in the mud. Then two hours passed. And I think it was after three and a half that finally I saw it. In the window. In the window on the third floor up. This light went on. This . . . this quiet, beautiful, white-blue light. Other lights had gone on while I was waiting, but somehow, this one, I knew. I knew this one was it. And I stood up, and I prayed, and I told heaven that if they just let me see him once more, I'd give it another year. I'd work and follow orders and do everything they wanted, just, please, I asked. Just, his face. And a figure came closer to the window. And I saw him, right there, framed in the most beautiful white-blue light. And he didn't look well, but it was him. And I saw him look up at the sky, and he closed his eyes, like maybe he was talking to heaven too. Like maybe he was asking the same thing.

And I didn't make a noise, not a sound, but suddenly his eyes looked down, at the alley, at the mud near the west side of the building. And he saw me, there, covered in mud, waiting.

And I felt the sensation of falling in love with him, with life, with this very strange, twisted, beautiful world, all over again.

LIKE NEVER

Elena's father is about to leave the house for good.
Very upset, Elena does her best to stop him, or,
rather, to make sure it isn't easy. She's a very strong
young woman with a lot on her mind.

Get out of your way? Why? Why should I? Gimme one reason why you think I should let you walk out that door. Go
ahead. Gimme one, decent reason why I think I should let
you leave me, and Mom, and Danny behind.

Why, because you want to? Go ahead, gimme a speech
about "free will vs. destiny" or something like I was one of
your students. Like I'm supposed to be impressed 'cause you
wrote a book about philosophy. Go ahead, I'd love to hear
it. I listen to your lectures all the time, right? One more's not
gonna do any harm. I know what it's all about. I mean, not
all of it, but most of it, I get it. I know what "free will"
means.

You think I'm gonna make this easy for you, Dad? You
walk out on all of us, you hurt us like that, you think I'm
not gonna do everything I can to hurt you too?

If you walk out and get in your car and drive to wher-
ever-it-is-you're-going, I'm never going to talk to you again.
And I don't mean that as some little-girl threat either. You
can't buy this one back with an ice cream cone or a balloon
or a trip to Chuck E. Cheese.

You can't buy this one back, like, at all. Like, NEVER.

No. I'm not getting out of your way. I'm not making this
easy for you. I'm not making this simple. You don't deserve
that.

I'm NOT, a simple, decision.

FOR LIKE A SECOND

A young woman defends herself after her little brother gets hit by a car.

I was just . . . I was just walking across the street real quick, for like a second, I was gonna talk to Stacy and yea, maybe I left the door open, but still, I was just walking real quick.

And I crossed through the front yard and Stacy saw me and waved me down and she was in the middle of checking mail for her mom and I ran across the street to tell her that Brett kinda asked me out today during Physics, I mean, he didn't, but he kinda did, and I didn't realize I had left the door open . . .

And . . . yeah. . . I kinda heard his voice behind me, I heard Jamie say something behind me but I didn't turn around 'cause I was so focused on talking to Stacy, so I knew he was behind me I just, I just didn't realize how close . . .

And the next thing I know I hear a screeching noise like tires and then like a thud and I know, I know even before I turn around what happened.

And there's this car, a Ford like Uncle Rick's, a Mustang, and there's this dent on the hood, and that's the first thing I notice. And the guy behind the wheel, he's, he's maybe thirty or something, he just looks straight at me, like terrified . . . like "oh-my-god-what-did-I-just-do" . . .

And there's Jamie, on the floor. My little brother, just . . . bleeding but not like when he gets nosebleeds and not like he scraped his knee like when he falls off the swings or the slide or whatever . . . He's just . . . he's bleeding.

And he's not moving.

And for like a second, I just, I just stand there.

And I'm just . . . frozen, I'm not moving . . .

And neither is he.

SUFFOCATING

A teenage girl deals with her father's overprotective-ness after her sister goes missing.

Ugh. It's unbearable. It's . . . it's suffocating. It's like he doesn't want me to go anywhere outside the front door 'cause that's like, the Danger Zone or whatever and anything could happen to me and he just, he just wants to keep me in this airtight bubble where nothing can ever happen to me.

I know the world sucks. I know bad stuff happens to good people all the time. Trust me, I know, it's just . . . That was Katherine, you know? That was . . . another person. It's not gonna happen to me. I mean, at least I hope it doesn't.

It's been . . . two years already. She went missing a year ago, they found her, they found her a couple months later . . . it's been . . . a while . . .

He should've gotten over it by now. I know . . . I know it's hard. I mean, I don't know what it's like to be a DAD and lose someone but I know what it's like to be a SISTER and it . . . it just . . . I mean, YEAH, I'm afraid sometimes when I'm walking to class alone or like if I'm in a hallway and it's dark or something but . . . But that's no way to live. I can't . . . I can't live like that.

Not every day.

I know it's not easy to move on . . . I understand he doesn't want to lose me too . . . but . . .

I gotta face my own dark hallways . . . Being afraid is something . . . I have to deal with by myself.

REGINA AND THE SCIENCE PROJECT

Here a girl named Regina defends a really badly put-together science project, one that, in the middle of her presentation, made the other kids in her class chuckle at her.

Look . . . I'm . . . I'm not a great speaker, OK? I'm not even a GOOD one. I don't . . . But I worked really hard on this science project and it wasn't easy and and my mom works a lot and my dad — he's not really . . . as "involved" and he doesn't — he doesn't know how to use PowerPoint or anything to make fancy presentations so . . . and my sister's kinda always doing her own thing, so, it might not be much, but it's all me, OK? You get me? ALL of it. This is all I . . . like you know how they say "do your best," and we're all like "OK" and we think we mean it? We say it but there's always something, you know, something you could've done a little better, but not here. I've never meant it before. And I mean it right now: This is my best. This is . . . This science project . . . MY science project, is really, really honestly, the BEST I could do. And when I couldn't use tomato sauce in the experiment I used ketchup and no one was there to proofread everything I had written so it's probably full of typos, typos I would LOVE to correct, but, no, fine, I didn't. Not yet. 'Cause this is me. No one else. Just. Me. And I might not be that smart and it might stink and be the worst science project you've ever seen but I don't care, and it might even be the best one you've ever seen — which obviously it's not — but I don't care about that either . . . and I don't want "pity," that's not why I'm saying any of this, I REALLY don't want, "pity," I just want you to let me finish my presentation, I think I deserve that, 'cause I know that no matter what you think of it . . . I don't care. I mean, I CARE, but not really. 'Cause I'm . . . 'cause right now . . . I'm really,

REALLY, proud of myself . . . And I don't care about the blue ribbon or the red ribbon or the anything ribbon, I just . . .

(She takes a final breath, with confidence.)
Detergent A worked better, OK? And I . . .
(Proudly.)
I figured that out on my own . . . Thank you.

PLEASE DIANA

Here a girl at a prep school has really humiliated
another, Diana, who has locked herself in a room.
The girl tries to get Diana to come out.

Please, Diana, don't . . . don't cry about it . . . Look . . .
Look I'm sorry, OK? I didn't mean to call you anything mean
I just . . . I mean . . . it came out, OK? You didn't deserve it
and I just said it and I was stupid and I'll even apologize in
front of the other girls if you want, really, I will . . .

We're not that different, you and me . . . You know
that? We're . . . actually . . . I came to Brooder Prep when I
was only like a little kid . . . my parents . . . they kinda
weren't . . . well . . . they weren't really PARENTS, you
know what I mean? And . . . well . . . This is home, get me?
I . . . I don't have much else . . .

Most of the girls here go home for holidays, or their fam-
ilies visit them, and . . . well . . . let's just say my parents
are generally pretty busy, so . . . "Busy." Parents' Weekend, I
normally sit under the bleachers and hide so no one realizes I
don't have anyone to visit me. Seven years of that, Diana,
that'll make you all kinds of mean . . .

I shouldn't've said anything . . . and . . . and I probably
only said it 'cause I wanted to look cool or something in
front of the other girls, which was totally just really stupid,
and . . .

Look, I don't even know why I'm saying any of this or
all of this but . . . I'd actually like it . . . if . . . next time we
had Parents' Weekend . . .

You could join me under the bleachers . . .

female • dramatic 69

DON'T FREAK OUT

A girl who died in a car accident comes back to talk to the driver who killed her.

Don't freak out. Just don't. Don't scream. Don't do that. Just sit down . . . There . . . good . . . That's more like it. Take a breath. Don't freak out.

We need to talk Marvin . . . Martin? Is that your name? Martin? I knew I heard it wrong . . . They didn't really say your name too much at the . . . at the "services" . . . it's not something they bring up, I guess . . . It's not like they were gonna have your picture anywhere near mine, near my coffin . . .

I looked good in my picture. They used the one from when I was in Florida that summer? It looks good. Did you go? Not to Florida, to the service . . . Yeah . . . I guess it would've been a little awkward . . .

How old are you, Martin? Twenty? Thirty? I'm not good at that yet. I mean, I would've been, but, you know, when you're young . . . Twenty-nine? OK . . . So I was close I guess . . . Close enough.

Don't . . . don't think I'm gonna haunt you like forever. I'm not. This is just a quick visit. Just one. You'll never see me again. I just figured, you know, I figured I should see you, see you in some position OTHER than sitting behind a wheel . . .

This is just a quick visit . . .

You've . . . you've become an important person to me . . . I mean, not in a good way, but, well, "a milestone" I guess, right? Beginning? Middle? . . . End?

You don't have to tell anyone you saw me, or we talked . . . You don't have to tell people 'cause they'll probably just think you're crazy and what'll that get you? Nothing.

Other than maybe some therapy and you'll lose your girl-friend . . .

I . . . I know you're sorry . . . It's not like that, either . . . I just . . . I wanted to see you, that's all.

I just wanted to say good-bye . . . And . . . I'm sorry we had to meet like this . . .

ANOTHER PERSON'S SHOES

A girl at some kind of orphanage or shelter sorts through donated clothes and talks to a friend about hand-me-downs.

Size six? Over here. Six-and-a-half? Over there . . .
(She sorts through more shoes.)
New at the shelter? That's cool . . . Size five over there . . .
Those are nice, yeah. . . You can tell someone's worn 'em out, but still, those are nice . . .
. . . One day when I get outta this place and get like a million dollars or marry some guy with like a million dollars? I won't wear anything hand-me-down. Nothing . . . Especially shoes.

As a matter of fact, when I walk into a store I'll ask the salesperson specifically for the shoes fresh out of the box, the ones that no one else has even tried on yet. Like no one. That way they'll mold to shape my feet and nobody else's first. They won't hurt when I walk and I won't have to deal with anyone else's shape, just mine . . .

It's like snakeskin. I mean, it's not, but it should be like snakeskin. One pair for one person. I mean, I appreciate these people and the donations or whatever, but . . . it's not right, I don't think. So when I'm done with them I'll burn them, cause no one should ever be allowed to wear another person's shoes.

Not me, at least. Not ever.

HE SAYS "WOMEN"

A young woman relives a choice she had to make regarding a stranger, this should be played like it's currently happening, present tense.

I'm walking out of practice one day and it's a little late but I figure it's no big deal and my brother will be there soon to pick me up, so I just wait . . .
And then I see, I see these headlights stop in front of the mailbox over there and I, I recognize the car, and it's Marty's dad, I know the car 'cause I've seen Marty get dropped off at school and stuff and, and I dunno like models of cars but I'm real good at remembering, and . . . and I remember this one . . .
And Marty's dad, he opens the window . . . And he calls out . . . But it's just me outside so I realize, weirdly, that he's calling me . . .
My brother hasn't shown up yet and here's Marty's dad . . . and Marty's dad is calling me from his car . . .
And we talk, for like a couple minutes, no big deal, nothing really important, nothing interesting, at least, until . . . until at this one point . . .
He tells me . . .
He tells me I'm really, I'm really not like other women he's ever met.
He uses that word. He says "women."
(A long pause, she thinks.)
And I feel . . . I feel wonderful . . .
And my brother's late to pick me up . . .
So what do I do?
(She's stuck, a deer in headlights, terrified.)
. . . what do I do?

UNTRUE

Lisa's father is a teacher. He teaches her friend. One day, the friend tries to tell Lisa that her father said some inappropriate things to her. Immediately after, Lisa confronts her friend.

Why do you have to make up lies?! Why? Why do you have to do that like all the time?! Just to make yourself feel better about . . . about yourself?!
My dad's a GOOD teacher. He's a GREAT teacher . . . and the fact that you would just say something so STUPID and so . . . so UNTRUE is just the most, the most horrible thing I could ever imagine.
Dad LOVES my mom. He worships the ground she walks on. And he loves his students, too, but not like that. He would never . . . he could never — . . .
I can't imagine why you'd ever even THINK he would say that to you, or mean it in any way that was . . . I can't imagine you'd ever think he meant anything THAT way . . .
My dad's honest. And smart. And religious, even . . . And you wanna open your mouth like that and just, throw his whole life away? And for what? For some stupid teenage girl lies?!!
He never!! HE NEVER!!! He . . .
(She breaks down.)
It's so . . .
(She's lying now.)
It's just so NOT true . . .

BACK OFF

A young woman in Juvie defends a newcomer from others who wanna fight her.

Back off, get away, you OK? You OK? I SAID BACK OFF SABRINA!

You can't do that. You gotta know that by now. How long you been in here, a week? You can't do that, you just can't. You can't just sit at Lisa's table if Lisa ain't tell you to sit there first, you hear me? That's not how it works around here, it isn't like all democratical or nothing, it's different and you gotta know that if you wanna make it another week.

Sit up, lemme see your face.

They got you good, huh? They got you right in the eye? You got that throbbing kinda pain now, huh? Like a sting? Don't worry about it, don't put nothin' icy directly on it, it'll hurt too much later, just put something, kinda cold or something, here, take my orange juice . . .

(She hands her a juice box.)

There, just put that . . . There, yeah, there you go . . . See? Vitamin C makes you better one way or another you know what I'm sayin'? Haha . . . Just hold it there. Yeah . . . hold it good, you don't want no black eye tomorrow, you don't wanna show that off, that makes you like a, like a kinda running joke, and you don't want that . . . You don't wanna give them laughs today and like tomorrow too . . . You just hold that and by tomorrow, trust me, there'll be someone else on the floor, someone else, you know, huddling over them . . . but not you . . . OK?

It's just like that here, you gotta learn, we all take turns . . . but not you OK? Maybe next time . . . maybe next time you'll be the one . . . offerin' a orange juice . . .

(She smiles sweetly, or, well, as sweetly as she can . . .)

NORTH BEACH

A young woman tells a friend why her little sister is handicapped.

You wouldn't understand . . . It was all me . . . My fault . . .
    When I was . . . when I was ten, she was about, I think
she was about two or three?
    I hurt her. Dropped her . . . Our grandma used to have
this porch, this, balcony-like thing? She used to live on the
beach, North Beach? Not South Beach, nothin' fancy, just . . .
just a little place, near a junkyard, actually, that's how she
got the place so cheap . . .
    Anyways, she used to hold her out so she could see the
waves, my grandma, she used to hold her out, little thing.
Two, three. However old she was . . . My little sister . . . So
she could see the ocean . . .
    One day she gets a phone call. I don't remember who it
was, but she gets one and, and she hands me the baby . . .
Says, "Take her, hold her close, watch it together" . . .
    So we're there . . . watching the ocean, like it's gonna go
anywhere . . . And . . . I dunno what it was . . . jealousy,
boredom, something, I was ten . . .
    I just . . . I dropped her . . .
    She didn't even cry . . . Just wriggled around in pain a
little bit . . . a minute, maybe two. I stayed there, staring
straight down, the rhythm of the ocean just beating away at
nothing . . .
    Grandma comes back . . . "Where's the baby," but she's
not asking 'cause she knows . . . She screamed . . . My
grandma . . . Not at me . . . just . . . at everything . . . The
whole way to the hospital . . . That whole night. And the
next morning, when they told us my sister wouldn't be able
to walk.
    You wouldn't understand . . . It was all me . . .

male · comedic

GABRIEL IS MR. COOL

Gabriel talks to his good friend, Zack. They're at the Junior Prom, and Zack is nervous about a girl he likes very much. Gabriel is firm with Zack, borderline mean, but he CAN be, because they're such good friends. Gabriel talks fast and slick, like a fourteen- or fifteen-year-old car salesman, or a fourteen- or fifteen-year-old James Bond.

Be smooth, Zack. Be smooth. Like cool. Like me. It's not that hard to do, imitate me. Half our school does it. Who started the collar-popping thing? ME. And don't act like I'm making that up 'cause you know I'm not. It's a family tradition: We invent cool stuff. My grandfather invented the high-five. I swear. You want me to call my dad? He'll tell you.

Look at her, sizing you up. YOU should be sizing HER up. Get over there. Offer her some punch. Ask her if she's having a good time. Anything. Just get over there, talk to her. *(Pulling him back.)* NOT YET! You don't wanna look too desperate. Do something cool. Lean against that wall. Like THIS! *(He does it, much cooler, to demonstrate.)* Pull out your cell phone. I DON'T CARE THAT NO ONE'S CALLING YOU, DO IT. Put it to your ear. PUT IT TO YOUR EAR ZACK. Smile. Laugh like someone just said something hilarious. Don't giggle, LAUGH. Giggling is for fourth graders. Chuckle. Like you're in a board meeting. It doesn't matter what a board meeting is, CHUCKLE. Put it away. You wanna look cool but not super cool. Yes, you'd rather be somewhere else, but she's not that bad. You never say "cool" or "great" or "awesome" you say "not that bad." Nothing impresses you. That's the message you wanna send. "I-have-cooler-stuff-to-do-but-if-I-had-to-talk-to-anyone-here-I-guess-it-could-be-you." And untuck your shirt, where are you, church? Smile. Not so big. Better. This is easy. This is gonna be real easy. Never mind, tuck your shirt back in, you look horrible. I don't know what it is, you just look horrible. No, not fat. I KNOW YOU'RE NOT FAT . . .

OK. Most important thing: Do a breath check . . . It's when you check your breath, that's what it is. Just like, act like you're scratching your nose, but exhale and cup it and smell, like this. *(He demonstrates.)* Good. Good? OK . . . There she is. You can do this, Zack. You got this. Be cool. On three, you go for it. OK? One, two, three. *(Zack goes.)* That's my boy . . . You should pay me, you know that?

(He watches Zack go. Gabriel looks around at the kids at the Junior Prom, all less cool than he is.)

You should all be paying me.

(He drinks his punch like it's a Martini.)

I give you people something to strive for.

DANNY AND THE PAPER FOOTBALL

Danny is a very confident young man who has just been sent to the principal's office. He's nervous, but plans on using his quick wit to get out of trouble.

I didn't throw anything. I mean, fine, I didn't throw anything, ON PURPOSE. At the teacher. I didn't throw anything, on purpose, at the teacher. Fine, but it's not a real football anyway. It's a fold-up one. A paper football? We — see: You take it and you fold it and you fold it again and eventually it becomes this triangle, with, with the thickness of cardboard and if you pinch the edges right you can get maybe ten to twelve feet of air out of it, I mean, if you're any good, an average paper football player can maybe get eight to nine — NO . . . No, I don't do this that often. It's . . . It's against the rules, which is really not fair, considering . . . Well, considering the amount of paper this school supplies. Or ANY school, really. I'm not saying it's the school's fault or even personally YOUR fault, I'm saying, I'm saying it's a problem in the system, in the whole school system, I mean, worldwide, if they don't want us to fold up paper and make footballs and throw them at each other and every so often accidentally hit a teacher, they should just do what any logical person would do and they would ban paper from schools. It's common sense. I mean, I'm not calling YOU dumb, not you PERSONALLY, but that's like handing a room full of preschoolers paintbrushes and paint and NOT expecting them to paint the walls — or better, that's like handing out knives in jail, or at soccer games in Europe . . . Look, I told the teacher I was sorry. I didn't laugh. Everyone else did, but not me, I was serious. My face was, like a rock. And, well, I didn't tell her till the end of class cause that's when I noticed it. It wasn't stuck in her hair that long . . . Forty minutes, yes. Well, no one asked her to have a giant afro of old lady hair to begin with, again, it goes back to paintbrushes and knives at soccer games — no, not paintbrushes, that was for the other thing . . . I OVERSHOT! OK?! Yes. I . . . Blake had the field goal set up and I shot it and, I underestimated my power, really, which, in the end, I think is a good thing, 'cause, I had no idea, I mean, I had no idea what my potential was, and well, this, school, YOUR school, the very institution you run, it helped me realize something very important: my unrealized potential. And isn't that what we come to school for on a daily basis anyways? To become better people? To find out something more about ourselves every day? To find out what we're capable of? . . .

(The principal says something.)

Yes . . . I'm VERY capable of serving detention on Wednesday.

THE OTHER KARATE KID

A young karate student talks lightning-fast and describes all the karate moves with accuracy and energy. He's not very good, but he IS really intense.

I've been doing karate for, for a while, for my whole life, really, since I was a kid. I'm thirteen now so, maybe, I think since I could walk pretty much, my mom says when I kicked in her uterus it was pretty intense, the uterus was like my first punching bag I guess, and I was born a week premature, and premature means I came out early, so a week early I was already like "get-me-outta-here" and I probably did something like a front-hook-roundhouse kick or a front-fruit-fly-bat kick coming into a hook-roundhouse kick on my way out, which was probably hard 'cause when you're born you have like this tube connecting your stomach to your mom's stomach, so that probably got in the way but either way I did it, which, I think, is pretty intense considering I hadn't even taken classes yet. It's like natural.

My sensei says I'm a natural, and I've never heard him call anyone else a natural, so I'm pretty sure he means it, though he doesn't say it around anyone else cause he probably doesn't want them to feel intimidated by my level of skill.

Which, I mean, is pretty high considering I'm thirteen.

I'm at the point where I'm inventing moves now.

I call this one thing the Smokehouse kick. The name doesn't really mean anything, I was eating at a restaurant called the Smokehouse and my mom's a realtor and she was talking about selling some house or something and I thought it up right there, in the middle of my baked potato, I was like, this would be a really good kick, and I couldn't come up with a good name for it so I just called it the Smokehouse. I drew out a diagram of the moves for it on the place mat in the restaurant. I threw it away later 'cause my brother got rib sauce on it 'cause he's basically an ape.

But he apologized a lot so I didn't do anything to him. Anything fierce, anyway.

THE CHEF

*The Chef is a well-dressed Hollywood-type kid. He's
seen everything, been everywhere. He's very confident
but lost in his own mind, a genius of sorts.*

"The Chef." My music name is "The Chef." I dunno, it
just . . . I call myself "The Chef" 'cause when I'm on a track,
you know it's cookin'. That's what my manager likes to say.
I think it's cheesy, but hey, man, if it sells T-shirts . . .

I actually dunno where it started, really.

I started doing music, I mean I started producing, I started
producing when I was like seven. Or six. Or ten.

I made my first mix-tape on a stereo my family had in
the living room. My dad wouldn't let me touch it but as long
as he wasn't home . . .

I held the microphone to the radio and like, recorded
songs from it and I'd pull it back and be like "yeah yeah y'all
you like that y'all" and I'd change the station and then put
the mic back on.

It was very . . . I was young. But now. I'm the biggest
recording artist under fifteen. And that's pretty good, I think,
you know, considering, 'cause most of my friends are like on
the lacrosse team or NJHS or something, but me, I, I'm a —
well, they perform at State Competition and I perform at the
Grammys, it's that simple.

I play guitar. And bass. And keyboards. And drums. And
I sing. And rap. And dance. No, I don't play brass, that'd
be . . . that'd be too much, you know?

It's a . . . It's a really tough life, but it's the one I wanna
live. Totally. Absolutely. It's the only life for me. There's only
one way for "The Chef" to survive, and this is it.

Music is everything to me. I wake up, I have music in my
head, my goal is, by the time I go to sleep, to have recorded
that song before going to sleep that night.

Rolling Stone called me a genius. That was nice of them, but, I dunno . . . Gifted? Yea. Prodigy? Maybe . . . but genius?

Come on, man.

I'm fourteen. Let's not go crazy, people.

CAMERON'S MOVIE PITCH

Here a kid named Cameron pitches an idea for a movie. This should be fun and energetic, almost like he's making it up as he goes along. At the end, the energy slows down a bit, as the story gets sadder, but then, picks right back up again.

I got this idea, today. It's an idea for a movie. A movie about a cactus. It's a cactus movie.

There's no section in the video store for cactus movies, I've looked (but there SHOULD be one, I think).

The movie starts: We see a cactus. It grows up on a beach, next to the beach palm trees, the coconut trees. And the palm tree things spend their days listening to the water, and watching the waves, and feeling the air push through their palm fronds, and staring at their beautiful shadows on the floor. And all they really do is say things like "Oh how wonderful our life is, we are like wonderful palm tree things."

And then there's the cactus, who doesn't do any of that, but he watches them do it (which is almost as good) and he thinks they're the most beautiful things he's ever seen. And they, they make fun of him, because, unlike them, he doesn't make pretty noises in the wind or grow coconuts, and because, unlike them, he has pricklies and it hurts to hug him . . . Years pass. It doesn't rain. It gets so bad the ocean dries up, and all the coconut trees or palm trees dry out and their palm fronds fall off and they crack in half and they die. Just dead.

But the cactus is fine because he's a cactus. But the cactus is alone, on what used to be a beach, right? But it's now a desert, now it's all like, *desert*-ed . . .

And one day after a long time of everybody being dead the owner of the world who is also a genie comes walking down the desert and says to the cactus: "Cactus, because you are so smart you are the only tree to survive, I grant you one wish." And the cactus says to him "Thank you so much, Mr. Genie Man who owns the world." And the man says says "What is it?," "What?," "The wish." And the cactus thinks, and then the cactus says: "Mr. Genie Man, my only wish is for you to make me a palm tree . . . " And the genie man does. And the cactus, who is now a coconut tree, lives for a day or two, listening to the sound of his palm fronds in the wind. And then they fall off.

And then he dries up. And he cracks in half. And he dies in the sand, next to the others . . . And that's the end of my movie. . . I mean you'd have to get someone really good to play that cactus.

THE SHREDDER

A garage-band kid with a pocket full of guitar picks speaks . . .

My band's name is The Dirty Metal Spikes. We used to be called Manhunter Deluxe but that didn't work out, there was another band in a town two hours away called Manhunter Supreme, so we had to change it 'cause they started their band like two weeks before we did. Whatever. Total technicality.

We sound like a little post-grunge, screamo, maybe some progressive rock sound with a hint of goth industrial. Whatever. We sound like The Dirty Metal Spikes, you know? I hate being labeled, or having to label ourselves. Like, these industry guys ask us all the time, what section in a record store would you like your records to be in, and our answer's always the same: You don't need "sections" if you know how to rock.

I play guitar. Lead. Sometimes rhythm, but mostly lead. I shred. I do a lot of shredding actually. We have this one song that's just me shredding. The rest of the guys go and take a break and it's, well, the song's called "Dirty Metal Shredding."

I've got a lotta influences. One of my main influences, I think is my Uncle Rick. He, he doesn't play guitar, he actually doesn't play anything, but just, I mean, he's a real influence on my music I think. He's been married like three times and he drives a Maserati . . . Major influence.

We're gonna open for Switchblade Razorblade Love next summer at 94.7's RockFest. It's way mainstream but it's what we need, I think, at least, as far as publicity goes.

And my drummer says they serve awesome buffalo wings.

So I'm pretty psyched for that.

THE "S" WORD

A young man's friend REALLY wants to go into a pet store, he REALLY doesn't.

I'm not going in there.

I'm just not.

I'm not afraid. I'm not afraid of anything. It's just, I don't believe in it. I don't believe in pet stores.

My goldfish doesn't count . . . 'Cause goldfishes don't count, that's why. 'Cause they have small brains, and my, fundamental issues against pets in general wouldn't apply if, say, the animal FORGOT, on a regular basis that he or she was a captive slave.

'Cause pet stores are cruel. 'Cause you got like seventeen puppies in there basically trampling each other, little cute golden lab puppies each goin "Aw, look at me," "Please buy me, not my brother," "No, buy me! I'm the cute one," it's sad, it's depressing, it's a living meat market. It's not like choosing a cantaloupe. It's different. These are living things, *breathing*, things, and you can't just choose one over another, it's, it's almost racism.

DON'T SAY THAT! DON'T USE THAT WORD! . . . The "S" word . . . yes . . . rhymes with "cakes," yes, very cute, don't say it — AGGH! — just don't SAY IT MAN! 'CAUSE THEY CREEP ME OUT THAT'S WHY! YES, is that funny to you? Does that make you laugh? "Oh, my friend's afraid of snakes, haha, let's laugh about it" . . . you don't see ME laughing about your . . . your faults . . . I'm not all like "Oh, my friend's got back-acne" DO TOO! I've seen you . . . then why won't you take your shirt off at the beach? . . . WE HAD PLENTY OF SUNBLOCK!!!

LOOK: I'm not going into that pet store because I don't . . . wanna be . . . in the same place, as those . . . "S" things . . . SAY IT AND I'LL TAKE PICTURES OF YOUR BACK WHILE YOU SLEEP AND I'LL PUT 'EM ON MYSPACE!! I WILL!! Thanks.

OH, KATHERINE

Here we find a young man who's in love with a girl.
Did we say in love? We meant obsessed.

Oh, Katherine, dearest Katie. How I love you! Let me count the ways!

One, I love the way you walk. So graceful, so full of life, your arms dangle elegantly, your legs sway one, then the next . . . everything else moves . . . just right.

Two, I love your brain. The way you answer Mr. Walton's questions in Geometry has wow-ed me since day one. The way you pronounce "acute" is so . . . a . . . cute.

Three, your flowing hair. It smells like flowers and sunlight. Not that sunlight is actually a smell, but if it was, wow, your hair would be it, not that I lean in and smell your hair every chance I get, I'm not that creepy, but sometimes in English I drop my pencil and have to reach forward to pick it up and — alas — the scent of your hair wafts its way to my nose and — BAM — I am indeed smitten.

Four, your shoes. The ones with the red laces. Hot.

Five, your favorite bands. I LIKE EARLY 90s POP TOO! WHO KNEW WE HAD SO MUCH IN COMMON!

Six, your singing voice. I know you're not in Chorus anymore, you haven't taken it since the sixth grade, but every so often, you let your voice ring out, just, by yourself, alone in your room, while you're doing homework . . . and I hear it, this pristine voice . . . at least, that's what it sounds like through the glass.

Oh Katherine, dearest Katie, "Kat," your mother calls you. "Kitty Kat," I like to think of your name in big, bubble letters, spray-painted on the side of a blimp, floating two hundred feet in the air, above the Superbowl, and I'm the kicker, and I have to make the game-winning kick, and I look up, and for inspiration, there you are . . . my dear Kat . . . And I make the kick. And I win the game. And I win your love . . .

. . . In my mind.

GREEN ARROW'S ULTIMATE AWESOMENESS

A comic-book fanboy fights a lesser comic-book fanboy.

Green Arrow's awesome. And you know why? — No, not Green Lantern, that's another guy, that's the guy from space. With the ring? No, not that guy. . . . No, that's Green Hornet, are you even listening?

ARROW. GREEN ARROW. Looks like Robin Hood? But not really? Yes, "arrow." Like bow and arrow and quiver and little felt hat with a feather in it?

How have you got no idea who that is? Are you kidding me? . . . I thought you were cool, Mark. I thought you were real about this, I thought when you said you were a fan, a "big fan" that's what you said, you said "I'm a big fan," you used the word *BIG*, and you don't even know who Green Arrow is? Are you kidding? Is this some joke? Some sick, twisted, not-funny-at-all joke?

GREEN ARROW! OLLIE! OLIVER QUEEN! Yes, yes his name is Queen and if that's funny to you I'm gonna drive this autographed copy of "Death of Superman" through your teeth, do you hear me?

I was in the middle of telling you how awesome he is, and you know what I was gonna say? Before I was so rudely interrupted by your unbelievable stupidity and poser-ness?

He uses his arrows, he makes new ones? Boxing-glove arrow? Tear-gas arrow? He makes them up! All by himself! It's like an unending power. And not only that, he carries them around, not even knowing when he'll need them! Who KNOWS what other types of magical, wonderful arrows he's got in his quiver — NO IT'S NOTHING LIKE THE BAT-BELT YOU LOSER!

IT'S HIS QUIVER! GET IT RIGHT! QUIVER!

. . . We're not friends anymore. Go stand in line with someone else. Go stand in line with one of the other posers who watches *Smallville* reruns or something . . .

. . . Pss . . . "Green Hornet" . . . Can you believe this guy? . . . Dork.

HOW TO MUG YOURSELF

*Two friends come back home way after curfew, one
has an idea about how to avoid getting in trouble.
The energy is frantic and hilarious.*

Just, just mess up your hair a little bit. Trust me, this'll work.
Open your shirt, rip it, rip the shirt open, I don't care how
much the thing costs, you can get another button, just, trust
me, do this . . .

'CAUSE! 'CAUSE if your mom catches us coming in a
half hour after curfew then she'll ground you, and I can't
have that. I can't have my best friend get grounded.

And not 'cause I care. Trust me, I don't really care, it's
just, if you get grounded next Saturday what am I supposed
to do? THE STICKBOY SKULLS are coming into town and
we've got tickets and you're my ride, and the only other person I know who's going is Charlie and I don't wanna go with
Charlie 'cause Charlie's girlfriend totally sucks and she's been
trying to get me with her sister for-like-ever.

So trust me, this works. Mess yourself up. Open your
shirt, we walk in there a half hour late, and tell your mom
we got mugged. Tell her we fought them off. Then — not
only will she be not angry — she'll be proud. Tell her we
fought off like six guys. They came up to us after the movies,
wanted our wallets, and we said no, we said no 'cause we
know how hard our parents work for their paychecks, like
that? Huh? Good, right?

Mug yourself. Just — good. That's a good look for you.
Now stand still.

Stand still.

No I'm not gonna take a picture, I'm gonna punch you in
the mouth.

'Cause ONE of us has to look a little damaged or she
won't buy it.

So stay . . . perfectly . . . still . . . *(He lunges back for a
punch.)*

THE CLOCK

*A young man tells us a nightmarish tale about taking
a standardized test.*

The clock's looking at me. At first I think, hey there clock,
no biggie. It's a tool. A machine. Like a calculator or a nose-
hair clipper.

I'll use it to my advantage . . . This test will be cake.
Total cake.

But then I look down and start reading these questions.
I didn't prepare for this. They didn't prepare me for this.
What the heck does half of this even mean? I flip the page
all frantic-like and the next page is the same. Stuff I have no
idea how to solve. Words I've never read. Things I've never
ever seen.

And that's when I look back up: Ten minutes have
passed.

I take a deep breath, tell myself, you can do this, build up
my confidence, do a sitting yoga pose, press my pressure
points, massage my temples, and jump back in, but nothing.

The test is still ridiculous. It's like in another LAN-
GUAGE. WHAT IS THIS?! I start freaking out. I can feel the
sweat in my palms rolling off and dripping onto the thing
they kept calling my "test booklet," now it's become my
"test sponge" and I look back up.

Thirty minutes have passed.

And at this point the clock isn't a tool. It's no longer a
machine. It's looking at me. It's sneering. It's angry. It's
laughing. It's happy I'm failing. It's calling me a loser. It's
intellectually BODY-SLAMMING ME AND THE CROWD
IS GOING CRAZY AND I'M LIKE NOOOOOO AND MY
FACE SLAMS AGAINST THE FLOOR OF THIS . . .
THIS . . . THIS STANDARDIZED TEST WRESTLING
ARENA AND IT GRABS ME AND GETS ME LIKE IN A
DOUBLE JOHNSON HEADLOCK BUT I'M LIKE NO . . .

I'm like . . . no thanks, Clock . . .

And I wiped my hands on my sleeves and looked back down at the first problem. And I thought about it long and hard . . .

And I figured it out . . .

And then I went on to question number two . . .

THE ACTION-FIGURE MONOLOGUE

An action figure complains about being, well, an action figure.

Look at him! Dude! Look at him using MY tank and MY bazookas! The traitor. The two-timing creep! One minute, "Sweeeeet look at what HE can do" the next minute POOF. BOOM. You're gone. Back in the bin with all the other old toys, with the old crayons. With the cracked colored pencils and leftover LEGOS.
LEGOS?!
I hate December. That's when the newbies come in. That's when the new-and-improved versions come in, shiny plastic packaging and shiny plastic skin. Look at me. I'm fading, dude. FADING! It's 'cause of the sun exposure. Jeremy left me in the SANDBOX last Sunday.
Can you believe that?
THE SANDBOX. I had to fight off two salamanders at the same time, while trying to find some kind of shade so my face and hair and moustache wouldn't fade, but look at me . . . LOOK AT ME.
How am I gonna compete with those? With THAT? The new guy's got spring-loaded jump-kick action! That's AWE-SOME! Look what I'm wearing. My camouflage is faded. And ever since Jeremy's friend Steve-o decided it'd be a good idea to do a Special-Ops rescue mission in the microwave, well, let's just say certain parts of me will never be the same.
I tried, I tried REALLY hard to warn 'im, you know? DUDE! STEVE-O! CERTAIN PARTS OF ME ARE NOT MICROWAVE SAFE, but do they listen? Do they ever listen?
Sometimes I feel like I'm not even here. Like they can't even hear me.
I thought I'd get lucky. I thought maybe they'd leave me in the box and I'd get to sleep it out for ten or twenty years and they'd sell me as a collector's item on eBay one day.
No such luck. Not for me. I'm not a Transformer.

PEP TALK

Sam plays for maybe the worst baseball team ever. He gives them, therefore, maybe the worst pep talk ever.

OK, group up, listen close.

I . . . I'm not good at these things, I'm not good at any kind of public speaking really but we're down seven points and it's only the second inning so you listen and you listen good.

Brett Gallager is on that team. Matter of fact, though he's the catcher, Brett Gallager is the *captain* of that team.

Nacho, remember in the sixth grade when you got up in the middle of World History to present your "World Leaders" project and someone taped a sign to your butt that said "Hot Buns" . . . that was Brett Gallager.

Steph, remember when Daisy and Dena got really mad at you 'cause someone spread that rumor that you saw them using "chest-enhancement" pills? That was Brett Gallager.

Max, remember when your mom and dad forgot to tell you they were going on vacation and they left you alone in the house without any food for three weeks while they were on a cruise ship in Alaska and all you got when they got from them when they got back was a T-shirt with a baby seal on it that said "You Seal my Heart" . . . That was messed up . . .

The point is, we might not be the best baseball team — matter of fact, we totally and absolutely stink and ohmygosh Kunal you're really much worse than I ever imagined — but this isn't about baseball.

This isn't even about Field Day, or winning the trophy or impressing Megan Mitchell who looks SO hot in that Field Day T-shirt.

This isn't even about winning. But I'll tell you one thing. This isn't about losing either . . . And we might not win this game, but you better believe we're not gonna lose by giving them a seven-point lead either.

Brett Gallager might walk out of here holding the trophy and even maybe Megan Mitchell, but I'm not gonna let him do it without breaking a sweat first.

We don't have to make 'em lose . . . but let's make 'em sweat . . .

SAFETY PATROL

A sixteen- or seventeen-year-old Safety Patrol talks to us about his (or her) experiences as, well, a total loser. CAPS indicate when he (or she) is screaming at fellow students. If possible, he (or she) wears one of those orange/yellow belts.

WALK! DON'T RUN! I SAID DON'T RUN STEVEN THIS ISN'T THE OLYMPICS. *(To the audience.)* Safety Patrol. I'm Safety Officer 1091077. Registered with the National Safety Patrol and everything. Six years I've been a Safety Officer . . . with the "Big P," I like to call it, the "Orange Force" or something, too, I'm trying to think up another name, something really —

— OFF THE GRASS! *(And back to the audience.)* I'm the only one here . . . there, well there were more of us when we were in middle school, junior high, there were even more of us when we were in elementary sch —

— WALK! *(And back to the audience.)* But the numbers dwindle, you know. People get other . . . "interests" . . . I guess. They sell out, if you ask me. Sell. Out. Track? Cheerleading? Drama? You kidding? When's the last time those clubs ever helped keep anyone safe? French Club? Please, they don't even get a badge —

— THE SIDEWALK'S THERE FOR A REASON TRISH AND YEAH I SEE YOU CHEWING GUM IN SCHOOL! PUT THE CELL PHONES AWAY PEOPLE DON'T CLOG THE HALLS THIS ISN'T SOCIAL HOUR. *(And back to the audience.)* The administration has asked me, on, numerous occasions, personally, asked me, to stop doing this. And I know why . . . I make them look bad. I'm a little more . . . how should I put this . . . "dedicated" than they are . . .

GET TO CLASS REGGIE THE BELL RANG YOU'RE
LATE WHAT ARE YOU DOING JUST STANDING THERE
LOOKING AT ME —
   (Suddenly the Patrol gets hit in the stomach with an egg.
Yolk drips off the safety patrol belt. He doesn't move, just
looks out at us and confesses . . .)
   Eggs. That happens once in a while too.

PHOTOSPOT GUY

A high school amateur photographer works at a lame PhotoSpot booth at a mall, and he takes his job way seriously.

OK. So. So just sit. Right there. Very good. Yeah. That looks good. *(Takes a picture.)* That looks great. Here, try moving, there, right, great. *(Takes a picture.)* GREAT. PERFECT. DON'T MOVE. Hold that pose. Stay right there. *(Takes a picture.)* Yeah. Great. That's beautiful. Give me "beautiful." *(Takes a picture.)* Yeah. Give me "intimidating." Yeah. *(Takes a picture.)* Perfect. Give me "attitude." *(Takes a picture.)* Give me "I don't care." *(Takes a picture.)* Yeah. *(Takes a picture.)* Great. Heck yeah, you do your thing. You do it. *(Takes a picture.)* YEAH. Give me "rock star." *(Takes a picture.)* You got it. You know it. Just one more second. Yeah. There you go. *(Takes a picture.)* Awesome.

(To someone who's calling from behind him.) Just one more shot. Please don't, please don't interrupt me when I'm working. Please don't . . . Just — no — we almost had it. Don't take him. Don't move him, NO! GEESH! COME ON LADY! We almost had "perfection." This was gonna be, this was gonna be, something! This was gonna be really really something!

(He gets screamed at.) Don't talk to me like I'm some kind of idiot, lady. I'm take Photography at school. I take "Advanced," OK? I know. Yes . . . Yes I know why you came here. Yes I know and NO, no I don't care. How about that. Huh?! I know you came for some lame Christmas-card pictures but that's not what he wanted. I know. I know he's three. I know. But he wanted more. He — I could tell. He wanted to say something. He's got something more to say than just "Merry Christmas" lady, but, you don't understand.

That $25.62 with tax . . .

(She pays him, leaves, he gives her the standard line, like a disappointed robot.)

And thank you for coming to PhotoSpot . . .

(Calling at the next customer.) Next? . . .

That's a nice cocker spaniel, sir. Yeah. We can do a whole session, just put him over here . . .

Oh yeah. . . *(Takes a picture, gets more excited.)* OH YEAAAAH . . .

SKIPPING PHYSICS

*A guy tries to get his friend to skip class with him,
and he then goes off about conspiracy theories.*

Dude, seriously? Seriously? Skip it, dude. SKIP IT.
Mrs. Henley's class? Come on, are you kidding? It's a
joke. The whole thing, man, it's a joke. Really. "Physics"?
Please. Tell me one thing, ONE THING, they've taught you
in that class that's really, actually, prepared you for the
future.

The whole thing's just some kind of perverse, hideous,
malnutritioned form of math. You know that. And what's
math? Another conspiracy. Tell me when you're ever gonna
use math or the Pythagorean theorem in anywhere OTHER
than Physics, and tell me where you're gonna really ACTU-
ALLY need to calculate the speed at which objects collide
unless it's maybe Math.

You know who uses that stuff? Insurance adjusters, people who show up after car accidents and tell you how it all
happened, people who sift through pieces of wrecked ships
and airplanes and can tell you, with precise and ridiculous
accuracy, what speed the objects was going, when and where
they collided, and what kind of mustard the pilot had in his
roast beef sandwich. And you know who else? And this, this
shouldn't serve as any kind of surprise to you, you know
who else uses that physics/math nonsense?

The FBI, man. Yeah. Trippy, weird, maybe even untrue,
but you gotta at least take it into account, 'cause that's the
reason this conspiracy of misinformed education really exists
to begin with . . . They're training us from birth, man,
they're training us, you think it's cute and construction paper
and math problems and how-many-pies-did-Sammy-eat but
no, no dude, not really . . .

They're making us little math-whiz-kid-FBI-agent-alien-signal de-scramblers.

And no, NO, I won't stand for it, I won't be part of this petrifying machine, man I won't, I can't, and plus, Tanya Pilner said she's skipping too and she's gotten really hot since the acne cleared up.

Blazing.

PROTEIN SHAKES ARE NOT MY THING

A teen tells us about his first time at the gym.

I went to the gym today. I went with my brother's friend, Marlo. He's this guy, he's kinda weird, but he seems really cool. I think he used to have a crush on my sister, or on my brother, I dunno. Either way.

We went to the gym and we "lifted." That's what he called it. I guess it's short for weight lifting but I don't think he's the type of guy who uses words or phrases with more than two syllables so, we didn't go weight lifting, we were just "lifting."

It was all going pretty smooth, pretty cool, until we actually stepped into the gym. Immediately I felt all eyes on me, guys wearing bandanas like it was still cool, eyes seething with Gatorade and sweat and steroids . . .

Marlo can bench-press two-hundred-thirty pounds. That's a lot. I . . . I barely benched the bar.

Marlo did a set of thirty push-ups as a kind of warm-up. I watched him, that was enough for me to break a sweat.

And then, then it happened, the single moment that made me completely secure in the fact that I'm probably never going to another gym for the rest of my life.

We were doing what Marlo called "curls," which is basically just the typical lifting of a weight thing you see all the guys do on TV, and, well, while he was "curling fifties," I was "curling fifteens" . . . But then, well, after two, I got really tired. So I started "curling twelves." Which, was also . . . a little exhausting.

He saw me struggling and he pointed me in the right direction, a smaller weight rack where everything was labeled with smaller, more manageable, even numbers. Six. Eight.

Ten. I could do these. I could handle these. I was "curling" in no time.

That's when it happened.

Mrs. Sherman . . . she teaches computers? . . . she's like sixty. She came up behind me. She wanted to know if I was done with the "eights."

Oh I was done. I was done forever.

LIKE PIRATES, BRO

A young guy describes the pirate-like freedom that comes with a new car.

Six cylinders, bro. Bucket seats. Ice cold AC. Feel that power. That freedom. This is it. This is life. This is what we were meant to do. Live like kings. Drive. Smooth sailing, bro. Like pirates. But in a car . . . and without swords. This is it. Pirates.

Chill out. NO! Don't open the glove compartment. It's jammed. Not broken, jammed, there's a difference. Broken means it doesn't work, jammed means it's . . . complicated. You could still put stuff in it, it's just, you can't really get it out, not without a flathead. A flathead screwdriver, bro. I got one in the back. In case. Just in case.

Sick dude. Drive. Listen to that. You hear that? No, not the engine bro. Keep listening. You listening? You hear that? No, not the radio bro. FREEDOM. No mom-screaming-at-you-to-do-the-dishes. No dad-screaming-at-you-to mow-the-lawn.

Freedom. Sick amounts of it. Dripping from our finger-tips, man. Anything. ANYTHING. The possibilities are —

— Don't yank so hard on the seat belt. 'Cause you'll BREAK IT that's why. Just don't yank it too hard, it comes off. It's not loose, it's just a little delicate. WELL I'LL WORRY ABOUT THAT WHEN I GET IN AN ACCIDENT, FOR NOW, DON'T YANK SO HARD. GET YOUR OWN CAR IF YOU WANNA YANK ON SEAT BELTS.

(A beat. He recovers, takes a breath.)
Like pirates.

NATURAL TUMBLER

A teenage boy has been forced into a sport he didn't want to join, by his mom. Here, he confronts her.

Mom. We need to talk. Yeah, it's about . . . yeah, it's important.

I was at practice today, and, well, Mom, I gotta say. I don't want this. I made the cut, yes, but, I wish I wouldn't have. Plain and simple. I love you, Mom, I love you with all my heart, but I don't care how much it matters to you. I don't care because these are your dreams. YOURS. And not mine, and no matter how much I try, now matter how good I am, I don't want this.

I was in the middle of a Toe Touch and I was just like, "Why this?" you know? I mean, of all the sports to try out for, of all the extracurriculars . . . I realized the only reason I went to conditioning was for you, the only reason I went to tryouts was for you, and there I was . . . and it all . . . it all just made sense.

Cheerleading is not my passion. It was yours, and that's cool, but it's not mine.

I don't care that my friends all made fun of me. I don't care that Nathan doesn't talk to me and Jimmy and Harold kicked me out of the band. I don't care that Melissa Davidson won't answer my calls anymore and Mr. Figueroa who teaches Physics spells out my name every time he calls attendance . . . "J-A-K-E . . . JAAAAAKE!!!"

It's not that embarrassing. All that, all that stuff I'd be willing to go through for you a million times over, Mom, I love you that much.

It's just . . . I mean . . . it's not my thing, it's yours, and if there was some elderly woman's Cheerleading Squad I think you should totally try out for it, not that you're "elderly," you know what I mean, bad word choice . . .

It's just . . . Left Herkie's and Toe Touches are for you . . . not for "J-A-K-E . . . JAAAAAAAKE!"

THAT THING THAT HAPPENED
IN OSCAR'S SHOWER

A young man screams for his friend. Waist-down, he's wrapped in a towel, and in pain.

OSCAR!!! . . . OSCAR COME HERE!! OSCAR CAN YOU HEAR ME? DUDE . . . dude . . . I need some gauze . . . GAUZE! Like from a first-aid kit?! Like the kind you use to bandage people when they're hurt? . . .

[Oscar asks why.]

WHY DO YOU THINK? I had an accident . . . AN ACCIDENT, I HAD AN ACCIDENT NOW CAN YOU BRING ME GAUZE . . .

[Oscar asks where he hurt himself.]

In the shower. I . . . I fell in the shower I was just standing there fine and dandy one minute and I'm conditioning my hair and no big deal and next thing I know I'm sitting on the bathtub floor staring at the ceiling and there's a cracked ceramic soap dish under me . . .

[Oscar: "What?"]

THERE'S A CRACKED CERAMIC SOAP DISH UNDER ME!!

No . . . not anymore, there WAS, I'm telling you the story . . . I dunno how it happened, I slipped . . . I dunno, I just did . . . Ceramic hurts. Especially when it's cracked and it's sharp and your skin is nice and soft and warm and you fall on it butt-first . . .

[Oscar laughs.]

Yes, I landed on it. On a cheek, I landed on a cheek, the left cheek if you wanna know exactly, man, it's not that funny. Dude, just bring me some gauze. Please? Don't make me come out there and bleed on your mom's carpet.

THE TWINKLES

A teenager describes the torture that comes with having the car for the weekend.

The Twinkles. That's their name. The Twinkles, my sister's dance company. Her "troupe," her . . . her little cult of creepy ten year olds in too much makeup and spaghetti-strap shirts.

And this weekend, Mom and Dad are out of town, which is awesome, right? Sure. Cause I get the car, right? Sure.

But my smile faded . . . MIGHTY FAST . . . when I found out what "getting the car" meant this particular weekend.

Yes, I could use the car to drive Ceci out to the movies and maybe dinner on Friday. Yes, I could even use the car to go out to Deer Pointe Beach with John and Freddy and them on Sunday. But Saturday?

Saturday . . . I have to escort the Twinkles to District Junior Dance Competition at some place downtown. And not only do I have to DRIVE four eyeliner-crazy ten year olds to this thing, this . . . hellish, freakish event that, if you trace it back, was probably invented as some sort of punishment for teenage boys in the Middle Ages . . . Not only do I have to drive them there and listen to BubbleGumPop the whole way there on full blast . . .

I have to escort them. Park. Walk them to registration . . . And watch . . .

(As if it's the worst kind of torture imaginable.)

I have . . . to watch . . .

GOGA-MILES

A young man who works in a video-game store tries
to convince someone to buy the latest and greatest:
DemonForce 3.

DragonsMouth 2 was cool, I mean, cooler than the original, but, well, you wanna talk about sequels that are just awesome, you gotta go DemonForce 3.

DemonForce 3 was sick.

If you're talkin' about a first-person-shooter that's just got unbelievable playability . . . I mean, it's the only way to go. Especially if you like killing demons.

And who doesn't like killing demons?

But if you get that you absolutely HAVE to get an extra memory card or two, and also you should totally get the virtual binoculars, it's the only way to play . . .

You can zoom in on them from like two goga-miles away . . . "Goga-miles" are the units of measurement in the game, in the world of Thandor, and trust me, you're gonna be glad you bought it when you've got a whole pack of demons waiting to attack you first, and you can use flame magic to ward off any evil spirits before you even infiltrate their fortress . . .

So yea, DragonsMouth 2 is totally fine, but, I mean, if you really wanna impress a girl or something . . . I think DemonForce 3 is your best bet.

SNEAKING WITH A CHAIN SAW

A brave kid watches a horror movie that he thinks he's too good for . . . he gradually gets more and more into it.

That's why I hate these movies. All this blood. Doesn't make sense. These things aren't even scary, man . . . What's scary about some serial killer with a chain saw sneaking into their bedroom, man . . . SNEAKING?! WITH A CHAIN SAW?! I can't wait till this thing's over. You gotta be some kinda IDIOT to not wake up the second he cranks that thing on, and, well, you gotta be some kinda IDIOT to actually get scared in these things, man . . .

Oh, that's hilarious . . . Yeah . . . just walk in . . . yeah. . . go ahead, innocent lonely babysitter girl, just go make some popcorn, yea, that's a good idea, pay no attention to the flash bulletin on the news about the escaped crazy zombie killer alien whatever guy loose in YOUR neighborhood . . . just . . . yeah. . . ignore the news . . .

Geesh, man, I'm SO over this . . . so lame . . . soooo boring . . .

(A beat . . . he kinda gets into it.)

Oh . . . right, suuure . . . yeah. . . like she wouldn't've seen that, right? Come on . . .

(Still getting more and more into it.)

He's right THERE! COME ON!!

(Getting more and more into it.)

HE'S RIGHT THERE!! BEHIND YOU!!! HOW DO YOU NOT HEAR A CREEPY ZOMBIE KILLER ALIEN GUY?!!! HE'S BREATHING LIKE SUPER HARD AND . . . Ohmygod . . . Ohmygod dude . . . No way. NO WAY DUDE . . .

(He gets more into it, suddenly something happens.)

AAAAGHH!!! AGHHH!!! NO NO NO NO NO!!!

OHMYGOD I CAN'T WATCH MAN . . . I CAN'T
WATCH . . .

(He covers his face.)

These things aren't even scary, man . . . it's just . . .
I can't wait for this to be over . . .

STUPID TREE HOUSE

A boy just turned thirteen talks up to the tree house where he used to play with his female neighbors, they won't let him in.

Madelyn?! . . . Tina!! Are you there? . . . I can see your heads, you can answer me!! Hello?!! HELLO?!!!

Fine! You know what?! I don't need your stupid tree house. I'm a teenager now, did you know that?! Not a "pre-teen" anymore, TEENAGER. I can read books from the TEEN section at the library . . . Hello?!

You know what?! I get the hint! I know where I'm not wanted. I'm not stupid or anything. But you know what is? You know what is stupid?! YOUR TREE HOUSE.

I don't even wanna ever go in there anymore. I don't . . . I don't play "House" or "Doctor" anymore . . . I don't do that . . . I'm a teenager now . . . I'm SOO done with that . . .

And Madelyn?! I know Joey Geraldo told Jennifer Gold-blatt that I told him I like you, but that's one hundred per-cent not true. Did you hear me?! UNTRUE! THAT'S A NON-TRUTH! MY LIKING YOU?! FABRICATED. I dunno by who, but somebody, probably someone real immature who's like a preteen or something . . .

You guys go ahead and do your talking, your chitchat-ting, your gossiping, probably about me, but you go ahead and do it. I have more stuff to do. If you need me, I'll be right here, under this other tree, but not in a lame "tree house" or anything . . . I'll just be sitting by the stump, like teenagers do, reading a book . . . It's called *Why Uncle Marlo Left Us in Winter*, it's supposed to be really good . . . Guess what section it's from at the library . . .

Madelyn? Tina?! GUESS WHAT SECTION IT'S FROM!!!!!

JIMMY THE CHEESE RAT

Jimmy, a teenage guy, comes running on holding a giant rat head, the kind that "Characters" wear at little kids' birthday parties. He screams at angry children.

STOP IT! STOP IT BRAT! LOOK! I'm only doing this 'cause my dad said I needed a summer job and I don't like the smell of fast-food and this lady Mom knows at work told me about how her son made tons of money doing this when he was my age . . . OK?

I'm not "Johnny the Cheese Rat," I'm Jimmy, my name's Jim, and I don't like it when people throw things at me, whether they're water balloons, slices of birthday cake, or . . .

(He pets a wound on his face.)

Bricks . . .

Now I know this might be hard for you to understand but "Johnny the Cheese Rat," well, he's not here, 'cause, well, he's not real. He was made up by some nerds in an animation studio somewhere in California probably, and, well, you watch him on TV all the time but that doesn't mean he's real . . . all it really means is you have "themed parties" 'cause you're in the third grade and so your mom goes out and buys you stupid matching cups and plates from "Party Superstore" and pays me a couple bucks to walk into your house dressed like . . . like an IDIOT . . . OK?

So back off . . . Go easy on me . . . This job stinks . . . But someday you'll understand . . . Someday you'll realize why it's important to have a couple bucks when the weekend comes, why it's important to be able to take Meredith Mendez out to a movie . . . 'cause she's got lips like a goddess and . . .

(He looks suddenly afraid.)

Hey . . . Put down the brick, kid . . . Put it down . . . PUT IT— *(But he gets hit.)* —AAAGHGH!!!

male · dramatic

VEINS

Martin tells us the story of how he taught himself to shave. He should remember how much this hurt, both physically and emotionally.

I . . . I used to get lots of cuts too. I used to . . . Tons of cuts. It's hard when you're first starting out it's . . . Truth is, I kinda taught myself. When — when I asked my, my dad, he told me men taught that to their sons when they were ready. I told him I thought I was ready. He told me I wasn't. I insisted, showed him my peach fuzz, told him it was starting to bother me and could I shave it and could he show me.

He told me I was no one to judge when I was a man. Told me it was up to him . . . Called me, the usual names . . . I . . . It's hard to explain, but I didn't care. I mean . . . I just didn't.

(A pause, Martin remembers.)

Something like eleven thirty at night, I crept into the bathroom. Found his razor, cream, everything. I had no idea what I was doing. Turned the water on real light 'cause I didn't wanna wake him. It was hardly running, it was just dripping, really.

Spent more time cleaning the blood off the porcelain than anything else, watching little swirls of dripping water into red puddles that belonged in my face.

He saw me the next morning. He laughed.

I didn't, but he laughed so hard. Called me — the usual. And he never taught me.

I taught myself. Scraping and scraping and shaving the wrong way and my veins just, tired from the learning, but, I taught myself.

Found my own way . . . Better than his.

THE BASEBALL MITT

Fifteen, this guy has burst into the locker room at school looking for something very specific, and very special.

Just look for it, man. Can you do that? It's here. Help me look for it. Black with tan laces. It's not just any mitt, Kyle, it's — it's important. Tan laces. Black with TAN laces. I know I left it here, I must've left it here. It's not in the locker room, it's not in Hugo's car, it must be . . . It's gotta be here.
(Searches.)
Where is it . . . Check — check over there too.
(Searches.)
I checked Terri's car. I checked under the bleachers. I checked the dugouts. It's dark but I checked. I got a flashlight from coach, I checked, but it's nowhere, trust me, at the end of the ninth, I had it in my bag, and now, now, it's . . .
(Searches.)
It can't just DISAPPEAR! Kyle, Things DON'T JUST DISAPPEAR!
It's my brother's mitt. It . . . It *was* my brother's mitt. Before he — it was *his.* OK? It was Charlie's . . . And I need it. I need my brother's mitt. It's not "luck," it's not a "luck" thing . . . It's . . .
(Searches.)
IT CAN'T JUST DISAPPEAR! Things don't JUST DISAPPEAR! . . .
(Almost defeated.)
Not . . . not twice.

TWENTY

A poetic kind of countdown, where a boy remembers his father.

Twenty years ago my dad met my mom. *Nineteen* she turned that day, it was a cheesy party cruise thing, my dad was the bartender. *Eighteen* days later he proposed. *Seventeen* people attended the wedding, nobody really approved, but they did it anyway, 'cause, my Uncle Charlie said to me once when I was like eight, "Your father was the kind of guy who held onto things he loved so close it hurt." *Sixteen* B, their apartment in a neighborhood that even now, my mother's still afraid to walk through.

Fifteen years ago my father found out he had this thing in his body.

Fourteen isn't the unluckiest number, but when the doctors finally had a name for it, it was that many letters long: "malignant tumor." *Thirteen* months, they gave him. *Twelve* years have gone by since the day I was born. *Eleven* years have gone by since the day my father went away for good.

Ten people in my life have said this really stupid thing to me: "Wow, looks like you just missed each other." *Nine* of those people I punched in the stomach. The other was my Math teacher. (I wish.)

Eight old rusty videotapes were in this box, I was moving Halloween decorations into the attic last night. *Seven* of them were stupid birthday videos, weddings, blah blah. Then there was this . . . unmarked tape.

Six minutes of static and then suddenly, there we are, my father and I, I'm like less than a year old. He's got me. He's holding me. There are nurses standing around him, he's in a hospital bed. *Five* times he kisses my forehead, holds me up to the camera, like he's so proud, like I'm Simba or something, only cuter. Much cuter. *Four* doctors rush in, some machine beeps *three* times in the background after his eyes go blank and he collapses on himself. They wheel him out of the room in a rush. For some reason, somebody's still filming. *Two* arms took me away, my mother's.

One time, when I was like eight, my Uncle Charlie said to me, "Your father was the kind of guy who held onto things he loved so close it hurt."

And it hurt . . . And it hurts still.

THIS IS ALIEN ME

A guy was out with a bunch of friends. One of these friends is a girl he's had a crush on forever. This is his first moment with her alone, and he's decided on talking about aliens — until something slips.

I don't see why. I mean, like if we're here, it'd only be *really* arrogant to think they're *not*, know what I mean?

I like to keep an open mind. I think that's what makes me different.

People think it's my car, it's my religious beliefs in the powers of the abnormal, it's my haircut, or lack of a haircut, but it's not. None of those things set you apart, like an open mind, man.

I mean, I don't wanna ramble, so stop me if you wanna, but don't you think they've GOT to exist? And if they exist, don't you think they're most likely just like us?

Maybe somewhere, on another planet, there's an alien version of me, and he's hanging out with an alien version of you, and they just went to the movies with a bunch of their alien friends and had dinner at an awesome sushi restaurant where they ordered awesome alien sashimi platters . . .

And maybe alien me is sitting with alien you, looking at the stars, rambling on and on about how he believes somewhere out there there's a "human" version of him, which would be me, but he wouldn't use the word *human*, no, he'd use some other alien word, and he'd talk and talk and not shut up, all 'cause deep down inside, he can't stand to be quiet around you. 'Cause deep down inside, every second he's not talking is a second he gets to think, and he doesn't like to think, 'cause deep down inside, he's thinking about how much he'd like to kiss you.

And he wants to. Alien me, I mean. He wants to a lot.

HOLD IT DOWN, THE BLOCK

An urban young man — hoodie, proud — tells us about his neighborhood, his world.

This is . . . this is the block. The world — my world, our world — begins and ends here, so we protect what we got, 'cause this, this is all we got, and nobody's knocking on our doors to give us anything else anytime soon.

Every sixteen minutes the number fifty-two bus stops here. It's mostly packed at seven in the morning and then again like around seven thirty, when everyone's done working overtime and is on their way home.

The ice cream truck comes by here every day between three and three fifteen o'clock. The dude that drives it turns the music down and drives kinda fast when he comes by 'cause he knows none o' the kids here could really afford anything anyways . . . and 'cause three years ago there was like a riot and another ice cream truck got jumped and the kids took all the sour candy and the soft-serve machine . . . That ice cream–truck guy doesn't come anymore . . .

Eight to nine people play dice, or dominoes, or cards, out here in the park in front of the building. Well, it's not a park but whatever. It's a something.

Ten, ten thirty, everybody's inside. Except the sketchy people, the people doin' stuff my mom doesn't want me to talk about. The people doin' stuff that gets them arrested once in a while . . . The people doin' stupid stuff that I swore to my pop I'd never do.

Before they caught him doin' it.

This is . . . this is the block.

I hold it down.

My block. Begins here. Ends here.

The whole world.

The whole everything.

STAY

This guy's jealous girlfriend caught him talking to this other girl. He tries to win her back.

It's not like that, I don't even know her, I mean, I know her, you know her, we know her, but it's not like I KNOW her, you know? It's not like there's anything THERE.

She's just some chick. And I don't use that word like in a sexist way or whatever, but it's true . . . She's . . . some chick. And. Well. You? You're NOT just some chick, you're, it's different with you . . . With you it's like . . . I dunno . . . I feel like, I feel real around you, like I can be me, like I can be, I dunno, I don't have to pretend anything . . . do you understand?

She's just some girl. She's a little crazy, she follows me around a lot, she's tried to kiss me like a billion times, but, well, I dunno, it's not what I'm about, and I don't have the heart to really tell her to just get outta my face, you know? I know how girls are, and, well, she wouldn't be the first to be completely heartbroken by yours truly . . . That was a joke.

It's you . . . Just you I wanna be around.

YOU'RE the girl I wanna talk to at eleven o'clock at night . . . YOU'RE the girl I wanna get in fights with about what movies we're gonna rent . . . You're the girl I wanna talk to when I get in fights with my dad. You're the girl I wanna think about when I'm in line at the supermarket . . .

Not just some chick . . .

You.

Totally, 100 percent . . . you.

I DON'T WANT NOBODY
TO GIVE ME NOTHING

A football player sits in a hospital bed.

So tell them . . . Tell them I said that, you hear me? I don't want nobody to give me nothing. It's not a party and it's not my birthday and it doesn't make it suddenly cool or necessary or anything . . . I don't want nothing. No presents. No cards. No flowers. No movies. No magazines. No candy. Nothing.

"Get Well"? No thanks. Tell them I thank them and it's nice of them and all and I appreciate every second of it, every dollar they're spending, all the time, but, but tell them it's not for me . . .

This thing, this thing inside me, this whatever it is, this isn't really mine. And I'm not feeding it. I'm not giving in to it. I'm not giving it chocolates or balloons or flowers or anything. I'm not giving it any more thought or any more time . . .

'Cause this thing isn't who I am. And it's not gonna be who I become.

Tell them I'm thinking about the play-offs already. Tell them I'm thinking about plays. Tell them I'm writing a couple plays and with the O-line back in good shape after last year, I think we're gonna make States. I believe that. Tell them that. Tell them to keep my locker clean and not put any stickers or flowers by it or anything . . .

Tell them I'll be back . . . Tell them I'll be back in no time . . . And take those cards back. You don't have to give 'em back, but just . . . just get rid of 'em . . .

This thing isn't mine.

AND SAILORS

A young man tells us the story of his brother, a sailor who is now in the Navy.

My brother went away, he went away eleven months ago. He always wanted to sail, it was his thing, since as far back as I can remember. I'd go out with him, we lived near the ocean, but, but it was always HIS thing. Not mine. Entirely his.

We'd ride out early morning. Every Sunday. Barely morning, really, it was the middle of the night and he'd borrow Dad's truck and he'd take out this boat that he refurbished completely, we found it in a canal by the house . . . We'd ride out before the sun even came up. He called me "first mate," not always, just Sundays. One day a week, and never in front of anyone else, it was like it was our thing, like he was seventeen and I was twelve and we were way too old to speak in secret codes, but we did it anyway.

I remember all of it, of course. Every conversation, every moment of every ride out to the middle of the ocean. We didn't go for the fishing or for the speed. We went for something else entirely. I have this one image, it's like burned into my brain, this one picture of my brother looking out over the water, it was an overcast day but the sun's still GLOWING behind the clouds, and it's like lighting every inch of his face, and he's baking in it, and he's loving it, and he doesn't know I'm looking, but he winks out at the ocean. Just once.

Like there's a joke the both of them understand. Like something no one else gets. Just the two of them . . .

He's on these battleships now. The Navy. We hear stories every day. Sometimes things happen, things blow up, things sink, stuff like that.

It bothers my mom, it makes my dad nervous, he started smoking again.

But I'm happy. I think . . . I love him and I'd love it if he came back, don't get me wrong . . . But . . . I know he's where he needs to be. It's something no one else gets.

Just my brother and the ocean. And me. I get it too.

RIVER MAN

A young man sees a mysterious man sitting by a river, and it makes him think.

There was a man the other day by the river . . . the one me and Danny go fishing at all the time? The one where we caught that big one last year?

There was a man there.

. . . No, it's not like that, he didn't do anything to us. He didn't even talk to us. He was just . . . he was just *there*, you know? Staring into the water? Watching it rush by.

Just *there*.

He didn't look poor. I mean, he didn't look rich either, but he didn't look like he had spent his whole life there, on the mud by the river. He was just . . . just a man, you know? Nothing really special about him. He looked regular, I guess. If I had to use a word, that would be it: regular.

He was alone. And regular. And he looked sad, and tired. Regular, though.

And, and I know this is gonna sound weird, you know, I know this is gonna sound depressing and stupid and stuff like that, but, it made me think, you know? It made me think about . . . well . . .

It made me think about what happened to him . . . Did he have a family, did he have friends? He looked like a nice guy, he didn't look like a criminal or anything, he was just . . . It made me think.

It made me think about Dad. It made me think about Uncle Mark. It just . . . it made me think . . .

I don't wanna end up alone. I mean, no offense to him, you know? But . . . I don't wanna be . . . I don't some kids fishing across the river, looking at me, wondering . . . at what point did that guy mess up . . .

At what point did that guy just . . . give up.

TONIGHT I LOSE THE WILL TO FIGHT

A kid who gets picked on talks about the last fight he ever got into.

They used to call me . . . they used to call me a lot of names. School was hard. School was stupid. I hated going. It was like walking into a zoo where they'd let all the animals loose. It was terrible.

They used to fight me. All of them. I was weaker. I was smaller. They used to want to fight, and by "fight" I mean they used to beat me up. I used to fight back but it just made them want to hit me harder.

My mom would cry every time I got home, it was like I'd just got back from war or something, she'd hug me so close, and it would hurt, it would hurt so much, but I'd let her . . . I'd let her hold me.

Then one time . . . I just didn't.

The night before, I looked at myself in the mirror, I looked at my bruises, and I said, tomorrow, I just won't fight back. I just won't.

Next day. They all came up to me, animals, all the same, they came up, they called me names, they tried get me to, but I didn't, I wouldn't hit back. I didn't even look up. They thought I'd gone crazy. They thought I'd really lost it, and then it happened.

One of them hit me on the back of the head.

I remember seeing the sky, then the floor. Then I remember more hands. Some punching, others grabbing, some clawing, some trying to help me, some trying to pull me away, others pulling me back.

My mom, at the hospital, when she walked in, she saw me lying there, and the doctors held her back, told her how many pieces of me were broken.

And she was afraid. She was afraid to hold me, even. And she cried. She cried the hardest that time.

REGISTER

A recently orphaned rebel teen living with his uncle's family tries to defend himself after the uncle accuses him of stealing from a cash register at the uncle's store.

I wasn't even in the store then! That's so not fair. I was out. Out back. I was with Jamie and them. We were outside, Frank got his hands on this sweet dirt bike and we were takin' turns with it up and down the block.

I left Steven watching the register. Steven, your son. I left him behind the counter and told him I'd be right back and yeah, maybe I was gone too long, maybe I was gone ten or fifteen or twenty minutes, maybe I took too long'a break, but I didn't take no money.

I wouldn't steal, Uncle Perry. Not from you. Not after all you done for me. Not after taking me in and your payin' for Mom's funeral and all that. I wouldn't steal from you, Uncle Perry, please don't keep lookin' at me like that.

Look.

I know I lied about stuff before, I know I haven't been the best nephew, I know you think I'm a bad influence on Steven and Beth and them, I know I'm more trouble than I'm worth, I know if I was just some kid on the street and not your blood you'd probably think I was some loser with nothin' goin' for him and nothin' ever goin' for him . . . I know I don't got nothin' goin' for me . . . I'm not smart or proper or clean or funny or even nice to people like Steven or Beth or you, Uncle Perry.

But you gotta trust me. I really mean this.

I didn't take no money from that register.

TANYA'S BROTHER

A guy tries to get his friend to come with him to get revenge on a bully that used to beat up on his big sister.

Ain't no big deal. He's just some kid. I'm not "bothered," don't say that, you sound like that counselor lady at school, whatever-her-name-was. He's some kid. That's it, and I need you to come with me.

I don't need no help, you don't gotta watch out for me, just, I need you to come, cause I need to do this and I don't wanna do it alone.

We're not gonna hurt 'im, not bad at least. It's just something I gotta do.

'Cause . . . 'CAUSE, geesh, you need an explanation for everything?! Since when you need an explanation for everything?!!

Tanya, OK? Tanya, my sister . . . When she was . . . geesh . . . when she was in the sixth grade or something, I was, maybe, what, fourth? . . . Yeah . . . the second time I took it, very funny.

I was in fourth grade and I come out to the park after school and there he is, that guy, and he's arguin' with Tanya or something and I'm not sure why so I run up and all I hear's a lot of screaming at first and she's crying almost not out of anger but out of like frustration or something and the kid's calling her trash, and he's callin' my family trash, I mean, nothing I'd never heard before from anyone else, but this guy, he's, he's really goin' off on my sister . . . "You're poor," "You're all trash," "You're nothing," stuff like that, stuff I'll never forget . . . then the guy . . . this kid . . . he hits her . . .

(A beat.)

He hits her and she's down and she's on the ground and

I'm runnin' as fast as I can and I jump on the kid but he just slams me right down on the ground and starts poundin' at me . . . and I'm . . . I mean . . . I'm little . . . And she's cryin' . . . And I can't . . .
    (He gets lost in the memory.)
    I can't . . . *(A beat.)*
    And I'm bigger now. Not huge, but big enough . . . We're not gonna hurt 'im, not bad at least. It's just something I gotta do . . . You comin' with me or what?

ITS RIGHT PLACE

A teen struggles with obsessive-compulsive disorder,
and making new friends.

That's not where books go — books go over here — books
go over here that's where books go . . . That's just where
they . . . OK? You gotta . . . you gotta keep order, right?
　　It's not a big deal. It's not a . . . I mean, people think I'm
weird 'cause I have it or whatever but it's not a big deal, so
please, please don't make a big deal out of it.
　　I've had it, I've had it forever . . . It's . . . I used to get
real angry when I was little and my parents would see me
freak out and, it's, it's not a big deal anymore, I'm on, I'm on
some new meds and hopefully it'll calm it down, but . . . but
still some stuff, you know . . . it lingers . . . That's a good
word. It lingers.
　　Look. I really like you, and not "like that" like you, just,
just I think you're very cool and I think maybe you and I
could be friends, OK? And I don't have a lot of those.
Friends. I don't . . . People think I'm weird. And it's not
even that big a deal, it's just, it's order, you know? Everything
has to go, you know, in its right place. If not, if not, I . . .
　　And books go over here anyway so . . .
　　(A beat. He closes his eyes. Another beat.)
　　I really like you and I don't want anything to — . . .
　　(Mustering up courage for something.)
　　This is gonna be hard. Just gimme a second.
　　(He drops the book on the floor. Leaves it there.)
　　It's not even a big deal, right? OCD? It's . . . I can deal.
　　*(A beat. He is really trying to not freak out about the
book on the floor, but he can't help it. He picks the book up.)*
　　Books go over here. *(He puts the book back where it
belongs, almost ashamed.)*
　　Look you can, you can leave if you want to. But . . . but
I'd like it if you . . . if you stayed.

WHEN I FLY AROUND

A monologue for a male teenage dreamer.

When I fly around the only thing you could see is the bottom of my sneakers. People stop and point and teenagers take off their headphones and tilt their necks and there I am. The real deal. Magic.

When I fly around the bill collectors and the crew-cut cops and the skinheads all hop in their cars and on their motorcycles and they all follow me for a mile or two and they all say the same thing: When he comes back down, we're kicking his head in.

But I'm gone, I'm like peace, and the clouds and the stratosphere taste like the frozen-dinner aisle but I keep going, I'm gone.

I'm like Planet of the Apes–style, wormhole-blackhole-whatever.

Something sucks me in and spits me out atomically and anatomically the same, just in another place, in another parallel universe.

And I come closer to this other, new planet. And the stratosphere and the clouds taste the same, but people don't tilt their necks when I'm coming down sneakers-first.

Nobody says anything.

Except for this one kid, eight, maybe nine, who looks up at me and smiles and as I land on the sidewalk and wipe the space dust off my face, he comes up to me, eight, maybe nine, holding a comic book and he shows it to me and I'm on the cover.

I'm on the cover. It looks just like me (only more handsome) and he asks me for my autograph and hugs me and as he walks away he says "I told her."

He says "I told my mom you were real."

THE LOOSER MY TRUCKS

The leader of a crew of skaters talks to a couple new kids who want to ride with them.

Look. This is how it goes.

You wanna skate? You wanna ride Crystal Park? Cool. You wanna ride the pipes 'till Security comes and kicks you out? Fine.

But you wanna ride with us, you got another thing comin'.

This ain't that easy. This ain't some speech you give your mom at the dinner table about how you wanna skate 'cause it's a way of life, this ain't some cliché crap you write in an essay like "The looser my trucks are, the more free I feel."

This is different. Riding with us? Riding with me? This is different.

Take off the fancy gear. I could care less who made your shirt or your sneakers. Stop sounding "hip" . . . *Sweet, wicked, dope, sick, nasty* . . . none of those make the cut . . . Matter of fact, it makes us dizzy.

And you put the video cameras away. No snapshots, no Internet posts, no show-offs, your friends wanna see your moves, they come here, they watch. I trip on another friggin' tripod and I'll break your nose with my longboard.

'Cause this? Our crew? This isn't what you read about in magazines . . .

My crew doesn't ride for fun.

We ride 'cause it's the only thing we got.

NO SPLASH

A young man's friend committed suicide a couple months prior and he's just seen his ghost. He tries to explain it to a friend, who isn't too receptive.

Look Jake I know what I saw, OK? And nothing you say is gonna convince me otherwise.

It's weird. Yes. It's totally twisted and it's freaking me out. Yes. But it's what I saw.

Right there. By the dock. Right there next to McCloskey's boat. Yeah. There. I was just . . . I dunno I was just walking . . .

'CAUSE I NEEDED TO THINK! THAT'S WHY! OK?! I WAS WALKING 'CAUSE I NEEDED TO THINK AND I'M THINKIN' ABOUT MY MOM AND MY SISTER AND SOME STUFF I GOT GOIN' ON AT HOME AND I TURN AROUND . . .

And I turn around.

And there he is.

Just . . . just standing there. Looking out at the water, like . . . like he used to. Like . . . like the last time.

And my mouth opens like I wanna say something . . . my throat makes like a noise like I'm almost forming words . . . but I can't . . . I'm trying but I can't . . . And I wanna tell him not to do it . . . I wanna tell him not to jump again . . . But . . . but nothing . . .

And he just . . . he drops. No splash. No nothing. He just . . . He disappears again . . .

I know it's weird and I was there at the funeral too and I know it's totally impossible but . . .

Please don't . . . Please don't look at me like I'm crazy . . .

BOO-HOO PITY PARTY

A young teen's parents are getting divorced, he gets called into a counselor's office to talk about it.

So what yeah my parents are getting divorced. Boo-hoo let's throw me a pity party, right? Let's . . . let's treat me like I'm handicapped, physically, emotionally, whatever, let's treat me like a "special case" now 'cause my mom and dad couldn't work things out, right? Counselors didn't help them the first time, but maybe me, right? What the hell difference does it make. What makes you think you'll work for me. I don't need help. I don't need to talk about it. I'm . . . trust me . . . I'm fine NOT talking about it and going to lacrosse practice and living my life all the same.

(A beat.)

Just . . . just 'cause my parents decided on giving up doesn't mean I wanna or need to talk about it, or my feelings, or how I feel about it, or how I feel about them — which is, in case you're taking notes, is really ticked off. Lied to. Sold out. I dunno, whatever — betrayed? Stranded? Forgotten?

(A beat.)

I mean I know it's THEM getting divorced from each OTHER, not from ME, but I . . . I can't help but feel like . . . you can't help but feel like . . .

(He checks his watch.)

Are we done here?

THIS CITY ... THE TRAIN

*A street kid talks to a pastor's daughter, stuck on a
subway train. He's seen her before, and he knows
something is troubling her.*

You must think, you must think that I'm like some kinda sin-
ner, right? Some kinda . . . some kinda trash like real goin-
straight-to-Hell type? You don't gotta lie. I know about your
dad. He's a priest, right? . . .
    Pastor, same thing. It's all about bein' good and holy and
loving and smart and stuff, right? Stuff I'm . . . well . . . I
just think it's funny, that's all. A girl like you and a kid like
me, I mean . . . what're the odds, huh? This city, the train.
    If all people to get stuck in a train with, you gotta get
me, right? Some kinda . . . some kinda coincidence . . .
    (A long beat.)
    I seen you get on the train before . . . I . . . That's how
come I knew about your dad. He . . . he talks a lot about
that stuff. I . . . I normally got my headphones on but sometimes I keep 'em on but with the . . . without no music . . .
you know? That way people . . . That way it's almost like
I'm not even there, right? People act . . . people act different
when my headphones is on. People act, I dunno, different . . .
Real different, like when they think no one's looking. *(Insin-
uating something.)* Even your dad.
    (Another long beat.)
    Yo, you . . . you wanna talk about anything, you gotta
get somethin' off your chest . . . we're stuck here . . . you
just . . . you just spit it out, OK? This ain't a fancy confession booth . . . but . . . but you got anything you wanna . . .
I ain't goin nowhere.
    This city. The train. We ain't goin' nowhere.

ROMEO AND JULIET
MAKE-OUT SESSION

A baseball player taking Drama as an elective asks the director of the school play to let him be in the show.

Mrs. Patterson . . . I . . . I'm gonna be honest with you . . . I took this class to meet girls. Plain and simple. Yes. I figured . . . I figured "Drama" meant . . . I dunno . . . meant Romeo and Juliet make-out session onstage, kissing Jessica Ferguson, I dunno . . . meant SOMETHING . . .
   But then . . . It's hard to put into . . . It's . . .
   (A beat.)
   My dad wants me to play baseball, right? Grandpa played baseball, Dad played in college . . . and plus, I'm a pitcher, and good pitchers aren't too common, and, well, I'm pretty well-built for it, I've got the wrist, I've got the shoulder strength, at least, that's what Dad says, and I trust him, but . . . but . . .
   I'm not saying you've gotta put me in the school play. I'm not . . . I'm not asking for a major role, or anything . . . I know I'm not great at acting or anything . . . Henry's good, Danny's good, they work real hard, I know, it's just . . . I . . . I wanna . . . There's . . .
   (A beat. He thinks. He articulates himself.)
   I like baseball. I love it, and I'm not gonna give it up, not for anything in the world . . . just . . . I wanna show my dad there's more to me than being a pitcher.
   I wanna . . . I wanna show him that his son is more than well-built wrists and shoulders . . .
   Plain and simple.

SAY SOMETHING DANNY

A friend has come into talk to Danny, who was criminally involved in some kind of car accident. Danny refuses to speak.

Danny say something . . . Speak. Danny, say something please . . .

Do you know what they're gonna do to you out there? You know what they're talking about? They're talking about trying you as an adult, bro. You're seven months away from turning eighteen but the lawyer-guy, he's talking about putting you away . . . and not juvie, man, the real deal.

SAY SOMETHING. You're not gonna say anything to ME then who you gonna speak to? LOOK AT ME AT LEAST. LOOK AT MY FACE, LOOK ME IN THE EYES AND TELL ME YOU WANNA GO AWAY, YOU WANNA GO TO JAIL . . .

He didn't make it, man. The kid, the kid in the car. He didn't make it like at all. Died in the ambulance, bro. You know what that means?

The kid's dead, Danny . . . DANNY. YOU KNOW WHAT THAT MEANS?

Your dad's here. He's waiting outside. He was here when I walked in through the front door, just, just sitting, Danny, just staring straight out. They got him in one of those plastic chairs in one of those grey rooms and he's just sitting . . . Staring . . . They asked me to come in here and talk to you, at first I said no, but then I looked over and . . .

He looks like . . . Like not your dad, bro . . .

He looks even more afraid than you are . . . He thinks he's gonna lose you.

(A beat.)

Say something.

END OF STORY

A young man's sister was killed by a drunk driver.
The driver comes by to apologize one too many
times, the young man confronts him at the front door.

I don't . . . I don't have anything more to say to you.

What happened, happened. End of story. I dunno why we've gotta dwell on stuff. I dunno why we've gotta talk about stuff like talking is gonna make anything better . . . Like talking EVER made anything better.

I want you to stop calling. I want you to stop sending cards, I want you to stop driving by and knocking on the door and asking to talk to my mom. It's over, OK? It's done. And I don't care that it makes you feel somehow better to talk about it or to vent or to sit in my living room and cry about it, I don't care that it makes you feel somehow . . . better to talk about how sorry you are, 'cause all you do every time is make my mom cry and then she goes through one of her THINGS like when she hardly talks for three days and then not only did I lose my sister I also lose my MOM and the silence in the house is like absolutely unbearable so I'd REALLY REALLY appreciate it if you stop coming by.

My sister's gone. It was an accident. It was your fault. It was whatever. You're sorry? Great. Stop reminding us. We know you're sorry like we know she's gone. My mom knows, every morning, when it's just two of us at breakfast, my mom, KNOWS, and she doesn't need YOU coming around reminding her.

End of story.

(He closes the door.)

BEATING MRS. ARKIN

A student confronts a teacher in the middle of class about her constant bullying of a quiet kid named Eric.

Mrs. Arkin? Mrs. Arkin? Why don't you lay off Eric for a while . . . I mean . . . you like, you constantly go and ask him questions, knowing, KNOWING he doesn't know the answers . . .

[She reprimands him.]

No I don't wanna sound disrespectful at all, Mrs. Arkin, it's just . . . I mean . . . It's kinda obvious that Eric's not the smartest kid in this class, and I'm not saying I am, I mean, I totally am not, but, all I'm saying is . . .

[She threatens him.]

No Mrs. Arkin I don't wanna go to anyone's office and no I don't want a detention but, at the same time, I, I just have to ask you to back off. Back off him! He's . . . I mean he's a good kid, I don't know him too well, we're not like friends or whatever but, I mean he's not the most popular kid, I mean, Eric, no offense, but it's not like your, your insults are just sliding right off him either, he walks out of here EVERY time looking like he just took a beating.

'Cause I know . . . I know 'cause I see it. 'Cause between third and fourth periods I walk right next to him on my way to English and it's just like . . . I mean he's not CRYING or anything but you just, I dunno, it's like he's got this look on his face that's just . . . it's unfair, that's all I'm saying. All I'm saying is, maybe you should back off and not make 'im look like an idiot every class period. 'Cause you're like thirty years older than him and I dunno if you do it 'cause it makes you feel good or you think it's funny or what but . . . but it's not.

And it's not fair.

And I just wanted to say that. Detention or no detention.

I . . . I wanted to say that.

UNCLE DAVID'S HOUSE

*A young man describes being in a terrible flood, and
how his uncle reacted to the devastation.*

The rain started coming and at first we didn't think it was
much, we didn't think it was gonna really be that bad, I
mean, we knew it would hit us hard, but me and Uncle
David, we, we never thought — . . .

I looked out at the street, my room was on the second
floor, and Uncle David told me to not come down once the
rain started, and, well, at first it all looked kinda normal, but
then I realized the street I was looking at, like the STREET,
wasn't made of asphalt or concrete anymore, it was all water.
And the same with the sidewalks . . . And pretty soon the
cars stopped driving by, and, and the only thing you could
see was every so often something would float by, a propane
tank, a dog, someone's toolshed, and the things, they just
kept getting heavier, which, I guessed, meant the water was
getting stronger, stronger and faster.

And I couldn't help it but I opened my door and went
back downstairs, and that's where I found him, my uncle,
and he was sitting on like the kitchen counter, and he was
staring at this little TV we had, electric, portable, the power
was out but we had this thing stashed somewhere . . . And
he was just staring, straight at it . . . petrified.

And I told him, Uncle David, we gotta go.

But he didn't answer.

And I said it louder, just like that, UNCLE DAVID, man
we gotta go.

But he wouldn't budge. And I stepped back like real slow.
And as I walked out the front door, as I let in all this water that
was rushing in by my ankles, he said a few words to me . . .

"This is my house."

And I never saw him again.

DARKNESS TO OUR DINNER TABLE

A young man tries to convince his mom to leave an abusive and troubled stepfather.

Mom . . . Momma . . . you gotta come with me. Momma who knows what he'll do next. He ain't like Pop, he ain't like Mr. Pucker, Harry's dad, he ain't like other men . . . He's . . .

He ain't normal. No one . . . no one who thinks about the stuff he does . . . for the amount of time he does . . . is normal, Momma.

I know the war messed him up. I know it messed him up real bad but that was him, that was him in that war, not us. And it's not fair, him bringin' that back here, him bringin' back that blood and death and darkness to our dinner table . . . And not just in stories, Momma, not just in embarrassing stories . . . now he's bringin' real darkness . . .

Remember the summer we went out to Pekslope Park and we lost that softball game against those people from New Haven? Remember those people? Connecticut people? Remember? We can have times like that again. We can . . . I know he can't control it but we can do that again . . . That doesn't just have to be something you think about and remember like "oh-wasn't-that-nice" that can be your life again, Momma. That can be TOMORROW.

(A beat.)

I know you love him. I know he was good to you once, but you . . . this ain't good for you. And I'm not leavin' you behind . . . but I'm not stayin' here another minute.

I'M GOOD AT BEING A NERD

A young man explains the importance of a video-gamer's competition to a friend who teases him about being a dork.

This isn't just a game, Mark. I wish you'd understand that. This isn't just . . . this isn't just some stupid hobby anymore, this is my thing. I know video games are stupid to you, and I get that, that's totally fine, it's not like you have to like all the same stuff I like, it's just . . .

This is what I do. OK? You got soccer. Molly's got math and all that brainy stuff. Everyone's got their . . . passion or specialty or whatever . . .

For me, it's different, OK? This is it. This is mine.

And it's not just some stupid nerd convention, I mean, yeah, it is, and I can totally tell that, it's just, I wish you'd understand why it's important to me.

This is my thing. I'm GOOD at this. At being a nerd, yes, I'm GOOD at it . . .

And all I wanna do is go out there and play and maybe win and maybe even get first place and maybe get put in some gamer magazines and maybe be famous for like a minute, and that's it . . . All I wanna do is go out and play and do my thing . . .

I . . . I've been waiting, Mark.

I've been waiting for this moment, man.

My whole life . . . This is *it*.

MR. WALTON GETS A VISIT

A young man comes to visit his father's former boss.

Mr. Walton? Mr. Walton could I have a quick conversation with you? I just gotta . . . I just gotta ask you a question or two. It's real quick. It won't take too much of your time. It's just one thing, really, and I've been waiting in the, well, the waiting room for so long.

[Mr. Walton hesitates.]

Well, it's just that I don't think your receptionist likes me very much 'cause she was trying to get rid of me but she wasn't very good at it, I mean, don't get me wrong, she was very good at being a receptionist, just . . . well . . . I'll only be a second, Mr. Walton.

[Mr. Walton gives in.]

I guess, Mr. Walton, I guess you're a real busy guy, right? So I don't wanna, you know, take you away from other stuff, so I guess I should just jump in, right? OK. I'm . . . I don't really understand how all this works, really, so, you know, forgive me for that, but . . .

I was wondering if you could give my dad his job back. I know it's hard, and I know that it's weird I'm coming in here like this, I mean, I'm just a kid, right? But still . . . I . . . I figured, if there's nothing my dad could do, I figured . . . I mean, I don't think you understand what it's like for us right now, my brother might be a little sick, I mean, nothing terribly bad, really, it's not like that, it's just . . . I mean, being sick is just cruddy, you know? And our house is nice but Mom says we might have to move, and I like my school, and I don't think we live in a really expensive neighborhood or anything, I mean, I don't go to school with *your* kids or anything, we don't go on fancy vacations or anything, so I don't think I'm really asking much if I — . . .

[Mr. Walton asks him to leave.]

OK . . . I see . . . OK . . . I just . . . I just wanted to know . . . you know . . . how it worked.

Mr. Walton if the way I feel right now, walking out, if the way I feel is anywhere near the way it felt for my dad, I hope he never ever gets fired again . . . And same for you, Mr. Walton . . . I hope you never have to feel this . . . this little . . .

ALLIGATOR ALLEY

*A young man hides from the police in a strip of the
Everglades marsh. He describes the place.*

There's a stretch of road called Alligator Alley where (if you
got one) you could drive in your car for miles and miles at
night without seeing another car but for sure you'll see the
white-yellow glow of reptile eyes all around you, like over-
whelming you, like telling you a bunch of stuff like "Yo
hurry up and get wherever it is you think you're going" and
definitely like "Yo get off Alligator Alley."

Some people use the word *marsh* and not *swamp* cause
marsh sounds less like somewhere monsters live . . . I use
swamp.

Swamp means rotting squishy earth.

Swamp means the fish are hiding from the cranes, the
cranes are hiding from the gators, the gators are hiding from
pick up trucks and airboats, and me . . . me and my brother,
we're hiding from everything . . . 'Cause we got to . . .

Swamp means it's a place where mosquitoes take up
every inch of breathable air searching for your blood. From
far away it looks like smoke to you but then you realize,
"Nåah, that's mosquitoes," and just when you think you
shooed the last one away another one sets her tripod legs up
somewhere on your skin and you don't feel the sting until it's
too late, you don't even feel nothing till she already drank all
she needs from your insides.

A lady at the church center said something about how
some guy or some people made God real mad once and God
sent bugs as a punishment. I dunno if she said mosquitoes or
something else but whatever 'cause mosquitoes are bugs. She
said that was over . . .

But after about five minutes here, after five minutes in
the swamp, you realize God's still like real angry . . .

NACHO

A young illegal immigrant gets caught by Immigration Police and questioned.

Ignacio. Ignacio Hernandez . . . Seventeen . . . Social security number? Lemme get back to you on that . . . My father? My father is alive. And Spanish. Not from Spain, but "Spanish" like you call it here, like from-Mexico-Spanish. He's a painter and a farmer and a lawn mower and a construction worker and a dishwasher and a pretty-much-everything-er. Only thing he's not is legal. Which is . . . whatever . . .
My mom? She's not . . . She's not alive. She peaced out before I ever really got to know her, so it's not like it's a big deal to me. It's not. It's whatever. It's not a thing. It's whatever. Why you asking such stupid questions, Mister? . . .
My sister. She does . . . I don't. I don't miss her 'cause I never knew her. My sister misses her like mad amounts, though, and my sister hates everybody so I figure Mom must've been pretty cool. Her and Pop fell in love like outside a movie theater and slow danced on the dock or something and got married at a church I never saw, called San Benito de los Reyes. That I know, too. The name of the church . . . If you wanna write that down in your pad . . .
They had me and they named me: Ignacio. After somebody's grandfather. And then she died.
You wanna write this down too? The suit was too big on me at the funeral. I remember that, it was my dad's from when he was young. That's all I remember . . .
We lived just us three. Me. Sis. Dad. And Dad worked. And it was just like . . . like one day things got dangerous. And one day we got hungry. Not hungry like when's dinner.
Hungry like when you can't take it anymore. Hungry like you start forgetting things.
Hungry like desperate. Something you'll never know, Mister.
How come you didn't write any of THAT part down?

ALIENS OR GHOSTS OR BRUCE WILLIS

A young man, adopted, who doesn't remember his past, talks about lying.

It's not lying like it's a sin, it's different with me, Mr. Brown . . . You gotta understand that. It's . . . Being adopted, having no parents, all that . . . it makes everything tricky, you know? It makes everything . . . like foggy . . .

Sometimes I think back and it's like I woke up here. In this house, in this city, like just a year or two ago . . . I mean, I know I didn't, I know I didn't 'cause the paperwork says I been transferred from place to place and all that but . . . Sometimes it's all foggy.

So every so often, when someone asks, I make up a real cool story about my parents dying in some horrible way just to see if people notice I'm lying. It's just a thing. To see if they're even really listening, to see if they notice . . .

They hardly do. I'm good. Even when I bring in aliens. Or ghosts. Or Bruce Willis.

They believe me. So I make stuff up. More stuff. I lie. Even when I don't need to.

Just so I could be good at it. For when I need to. And they don't flinch. And I don't flinch. It's something you learn . . . You could do a lie-detector-thing on me and nothing. I mean, maybe something, I'm not a robot, but that don't mean I'm not good . . .

(A beat.)

I'm not proud of it, it's just . . . something you learn.

M. RAMIREZ is a playwright from Miami, Florida. He holds a degree in Dramatic Writing from NYU's Tisch School of the Arts, and he is currently working on another series of mono-logue books for Smith and Kraus. He's also working on a play about a giant.